Culture + Leisure Services
Red Doles Lane
Huddersfield, West Yorks. HD21YF

D1189213

THE BOOK OF
Margery Kempe

PETER LANG
New York • Washington, D.C./Baltimore • Bern
Frankfurt am Main • Berlin • Brussels • Vienna • Oxford

MAREA MITCHELL

THE BOOK OF Margery Kempe

SCHOLARSHIP,

COMMUNITY,

& CRITICISM

PETER LANG
New York • Washington, D.C./Baltimore • Bern
Frankfurt am Main • Berlin • Brussels • Vienna • Oxford

Library of Congress Cataloging-in-Publication Data

Mitchell, Marea.
The book of Margery Kempe:
scholarship, community, and criticism / Marea Mitchell.
p. cm.
Includes bibliographical references and index.
1. Kempe, Margery, b. ca. 1373. Book of Margery Kempe.
2. Kempe, Margery, b. ca. 1373—Criticism and interpretation—History.
3. Christian literature, English (Middle)—History and criticism—Theory, etc.
4. Christian women—Religious life—England—Historiography. 5. Feminism
and literature—England—Historiography. 6. Dissenters, Religious—
England—Historiography. 7. Women and literature—England—
Historiography. 8. Mysticism—England—Historiography. I. Title.
PR2007.K4Z783   248.2'2'092—dc22   2004015775
ISBN 0-8204-7451-7

Bibliographic information published by **Die Deutsche Bibliothek**.
Die Deutsche Bibliothek lists this publication in the "Deutsche
Nationalbibliografie"; detailed bibliographic data is available
on the Internet at http://dnb.ddb.de/.

Cover design by Lisa Barfield

The paper in this book meets the guidelines for permanence and durability
of the Committee on Production Guidelines for Book Longevity
of the Council of Library Resources.

© 2005 Peter Lang Publishing, Inc., New York
275 Seventh Avenue, 28th Floor, New York, NY 10001
www.peterlangusa.com

Printed in the United States of America

for

Douglas and Joan Mitchell

✠ Table of Contents

Preface

Researching and writing this book have taken me to many different places, to King's Lynn, Bryn Mawr College, the Northamptonshire Record Office, the Bodleian Library, the British Library, and the State Library of New South Wales. There have been many journeys, physical and intellectual, long plane trips, and long train trips by the Hawksbury river, and back to Cornwall. During that time, I have been asked many different kinds of questions about earlier versions of the work presented here. I mention two of them to illustrate some of the concerns of this book.

First, I have been asked what difference it would make if it were discovered that *The Book of Margery Kempe* were a spoof by a male cleric. Second, why didn't I describe Hope Allen, the identifier of the Kempe manuscript, as a lesbian? These two quite different questions identify for me some of the parameters of discussion about the *Book*—the first because it speaks from a tendency to deny women's voices and the second because it speaks for a woman in a way that she did not speak for herself. The politics of both seem to me presumptous, and both, in very different ways, refuse to hear the voices of women as they are presented. The first question denies a woman's speech when there is no particular evidence for doing so, and the second positions a woman in ways other than she chose to position herself. Yet while they converge in this sense, the gap between the questions also illustrates how the interests of criticism have changed. This book is partly an attempt to explore how these very different kinds of questions illustrate shifting debates about the *Book* and to suggest how they can be said to articulate understandings about scholarship, community, and criticism in the last seventy years.

The suggestion that Kempe might not have 'written' the *Book* is recognisable, of course, as a standard line of attack on women's writing in its denial of agency.[1] So unthinkable is it that women might produce texts that some other explanation must be found—an unseen male writer behind the arras. The eccentricity of women having anything significant to say has such a long history that even Kempe herself confronted it. When requesting an audience with Richard Caistor, Vicar of St. Stephen's Church to discuss the love of God, Kempe received an illuminating response:

> He, lyftyng up hys handys & blyssyng hym seyd, 'Benedicte. What cowd a woman ocupyn an owyr er tweyn owyrs in þe lofe of owyr Lord? I xal neuyr ete mete tyl I wete what ȝe kan sey of owyr Lord God þe tyme of on owyr.'[2]

> (He, lifting up his hands and blessing himself said, 'Bless you! How could a woman occupy one or two hours on the love of God? I shall never eat meat until I know what you can say about our Lord God that will take an hour.')[3]

Perhaps this scepticism is to be expected in the fifteenth century. How much harder is it to take in the twenty-first century? In the first English translation of Simone de Beauvoir's *The Second Sex*, the translator H. M. Parshley in 1953 wrote:

> A serious, all inclusive, and uninhibited work on woman by a woman of wit and learning! What, I had often thought, could be more desirable and yet less to be expected? When I was asked, some three years ago, to read Mlle Simone de Beauvoir's *Le Deuxième Sexe*...I was not long in realising that the unexpected had happened.[4]

One of the things that I am interested in charting in this book is the kind of criticism in the early history of Kempe studies that was profoundly concerned with the issue of authenticity, of whether or not she 'rings true' as a mystic.[5] It is the eccentricity of Kempe that often concerns bemused commentators, in awe at the kind of talking dog phenomenon that Kempe's own original audience is described as displaying.

Another aspect of this questioning of Kempe's responsibility for the text also undermines the credibility of the researcher in its implication that one is unable to detect fraud when it smacks one on the nose. Both aspects of this first question attack women's ability to write, think, and speak anything worth hearing or reading. If it is sobering to realise how long this attitude has been in circulation, then at least there has been time to develop counter arguments. Women did speak out, did write, and did research—Shakespeare did have sisters.

The second query is more difficult to deal with in so far as it arises from positions within feminist criticism and is based on legitimate endeavours to re-write women's history in ways that acknowledge women's lives, experiences, and lived pasts, and I tackle it here with some trepidation. One of the most enjoyable aspects of researching this book has been the journeys taken into archives of women scholars—a journey begun in reading John C. Hirsh's biography of Hope Emily Allen. Anybody reading the Early English Text Society's (EETS) edition of *The Book of Margery Kempe* cannot fail to be intrigued by Allen's references to forthcoming work that she intended to produce as a second volume on Kempe for EETS, and Hirsh's book is very significant for its interest in documenting the life of an early medieval English scholar.[6] The identification of Allen's rôle in the establishment of Kempe studies, which have now become part of the canon of English literary studies, is an important part of understanding how scholarship and criticism are produced in all their culturally material contexts.[7] To focus on the scholarship and the cultural production of criticism rather than focusing on the texts alone, I argue here, is crucial to an understanding of how texts come to have meaning in any particular cultural formation. For me this is an important part of a feminist literary criticism that does more than excavate women from history to supply a tradition of 'good women' for modern interests and values.[8] To put Allen and her community of scholars back into the picture seems to me a useful extension of the politics of feminist criticism.

However, as the tradition of questioning women's contributions to culture evacuates women from cultural production, the opposite danger is of reifying women and female sexuality at the cost once again of ignoring their intellectual labour. Just as the concentration on the *Book* as an autobiography that can tell us about the real life of a fifteenth-century English woman marginalises the effort and strategies of the book as a piece of self-authorising propaganda, so to position Allen in terms of any claims about her sexuality would be, it seems to me, to marginalise exactly what Allen spent most of her life trying to achieve— intellectual scholarship of a productive and lasting kind. Certainly Allen worked with other women scholars and certainly those relationships were warm and close, and to acknowledge this is an important part of giving women's work and women's relationships with other women their proper and neglected space. To claim more about these women's lives would be speculation and to seek attention for a criticism operating in bad faith. It is no part of my intention to dismiss work on women's sexuality. I simply suggest that in this case it is inappropriate. Allen was careful of her own privacy. To position her in terms that are familiar to twenty-first-century feminist criticism without acknowledging the ways that she chose to present herself is to risk the distortions of presentism that it is an aim of this book to avoid.

One of the things that have been important to me in writing this book has been the attempt to allow other periods and values to speak in their own words. While I am not interested in adopting any tone of impartiality nor in denying my own values and interest—which have of course brought me to this text and this approach to this text as I hope I make clear—it is also important to me to articulate historical differences.[9] As a cultural materialist, at least part of my aim is to be more aware of possibilities and alternatives so that we might better produce change. I hope that this book contributes to debates about how to study historically distant texts and how to acknowledge the work of scholarship in the construction of those debates.

I am very grateful to all those who made available archival material and helped me with it. First, I thank Wilber Allen and the Allen family for permission to quote from the Hope Emily Allen Papers held in the Special Collections at Bryn Mawr College, Pennsylvania. I also thank the following people at Bryn Mawr College: Mary Patterson McPherson (President of Bryn Mawr College), Leo Dolenski, and Lorett Treese, and Valencia Powell at Dolwen House. Professor John C. Hirsh at Georgetown University was also very helpful in relation to archival material. At the British Library, Hilton Kelliher (Curator of Western Manuscripts) gave me access to B. L. Additional MS 61823 and was generous with his time in discussion of the ms's provenance. Staff in Duke Humfrey's Library at the Bodleian, especially Steven Tomlinson, kindly located the Allen correspondence and identified and gave me access to new material, now MS English Letters d. 268. Debbie Gillings, at the State Library of New South Wales, saved me precious time. Jill Walker, at Lynn Museum, and Roy Smith, at the Townhouse Museum, in Lynn, were also kind enough to help with research in King's Lynn. Library staff, particularly in Inter Library Loans, at Macquarie University again helped this work. Rachel Watson, at Northamptonshire Record Office, shared her own knowledge of Joan Wake with me, and together with other staff there, especially the archivists Eleanor Winyard and Chris Smith, and Leslie C. Skelton (Secretary of the Northamptonshire Record Society), helped me through the extensive material held there. Peter Moyse A. R. P. S. laboured through snow and bad weather to reproduce photographs for me. I thank Sarah Bridges, the current County Archivist for permission to quote from the Joan Wake Collection and to reproduce the photographs here. I am glad to thank Richard Hamer and The Council of the Early English Text Society for permission to quote from their edition of *The Book of Margery Kempe*.

Some parts of chapter 3 appeared in "'The Ever-Growing Army of Serious Girl Students": The Legacy of Hope Emily Allen,' *Medieval Feminist Forum*, No. 31, Spring 2001, and I thank Gina Psaki and *MFF* for permission to quote. Some ideas presented in chapter 8 appeared in *Maistresse of My Wit: Medieval Women and Modern Scholarship*, eds. Lousie d'Arcens and Juanita de Ruys (Turnhout, Belgium: Brepols, 2004), and permission to reprint is gratefully acknowledged.

At various times, many colleagues have listened with patience to parts of this and read through drafts. Among them I would like to thank, particularly, David Matthews, Wayne McKenna, Jane O'Sullivan, Ali Lavau, Tom Burvill, Joan Kirkby, Bernard Martin, Marie-Louise Claflin, Ruth Waterhouse, John Stephens, and the Literature and Cultural History Group at Macquarie University. A. D. Cousins and Peter Goodall were particularly helpful and supportive throughout this work. Also, I would like to thank the constructive early anonymous readers. I am very grateful to Phyllis Korper, Bernadette Shade and Peter Lang for publishing this book. Macquarie University provided time and money to carry out research and writing through its Outside Study Program and research grants. Alana Sharp was always helpful and conscientious. Friends have given other kinds of support for which I thank them: Lloyd, Paula, Max and Caitlin Clark; Carolyn, Brett, Dalton and Annerley West, Jill and Bruce Bough, Tessa Morrison and John Burgess. My family—the tribe—have provided the kind of continuous support that is beyond price: Douglas and Joan Mitchell; Les Mitchell and Pat Usher; Jenny and Michael Thompson; Jill, Katrina and Nikki Mitchell; Robert Newhouse, and Bryony Newhouse; Andy, Julie, Beth and Sam Mitchell; Anna, James and Ben Handley; Jean Mackie, and Keith Mackie. Much as I am indebted to all these people, two others gave me very special help. Dianne Osland exemplifies the concept of friendship and combines this with constructive criticism. Robert Mackie is critic and partner, political and intellectual, realist and optimist.

Notes

1. Joanna Russ, *How to Suppress Women's Writing* (London: The Women's Press, 1984) p. 20, describes this as the first line of defence of the dominant white middle-class male literary establishment. It could also be seen as the first line of attack. I have put 'written' in quotation marks to recognise that scribes rather than Kempe actually committed the words to paper and that what is at stake here is responsibility for the content of the text.

2. *The Book of Margery Kempe*, ed. Sanford Brown Meech with Prefatory Note by Hope Emily Allen (Oxford: Early English Text Society, Oxford University Press, 1940) p. 38:24–28. All future references are included parenthetically.

3. All translations are mine, produced with particular reference to the the EETS edition and *The Book of Margery Kempe*, ed. Barry Windeatt (Harlow, Essex: Pearson Education Ltd., 2000).

4. Simone de Beauvoir, *The Second Sex*, trans. and ed. H. M. Parshley (Harmondsworth: Penguin, 1972) p. 7.

5.   Very Rev. W. R. Inge, *Mysticism in Religion* (London: Hutchinson and Co. Ltd., 1947) p. 11.

6.   My work here is indebted to Hirsh's biography, *Hope Emily Allen: Medieval Scholarship and Feminism* (Norman, Oklahoma: Pilgrim Books, 1988). There are inevitably some elements of Allen's life covered by Hirsh that I allude to here, but where Hirsh's work is a biography, the purpose here is to include Allen as part of the history of scholarship on *The Book of Margery Kempe* and its cultural production.

7.   See *The Cambridge Companion to Medieval Women's Writing*, eds. Carolyn Dinshaw and David Wallace (Cambridge: Cambridge University Press, 2003) p. 222.

8.   See Jonathan Goldberg, *Desiring Women Writing: English Renaissance Examples* (Stanford, California: Stanford University Press, 1997) p. 11, and Allen J. Frantzen, 'When Women Aren't Enough,' *Speculum* 68, 1993, pp. 445–471.

9.   The attempt to think through the relationships between medieval texts and modern scholarship is the concern of *Maistresse of My Wit: Medieval Women and Modern Scholars*, eds. Louise d'Arcens and Juanita de Ruys (Brepols, 2004) to which I contributed a chapter, 'Uncanny Dialogues: "The Journal of Mistress Joan Martyn" and *The Book of Margery Kempe*' (Turnhout, Belgium: Brepols, 2004) pp. 247–66.

Chapter 1

Discovering *The Book of Margery Kempe*

On one occasion, probably in 1434, Margery Kempe found herself at dinner in London with a group of people to whom she was not known. During the merriment, the other diners celebrate a joke going the rounds: 'fals flesch, þu xalt ete non heryng.'[1] This is by way of being 'a maner of prouerbe a ȝen hir' (244:5–6) designed to indicate her hypocrisy, based on the idea that she justifies a desire for better food with the pretence that she is mortifying the flesh through denying herself what she really wants. Kempe accosts the assembly with the argument that they should only speak of what they know and not the worst of that. As they cannot have known her, as her presence unrecognised at the meal indicates, they should not talk about what they do not know.

> "Lo, serys," sche seyd, "ȝe awt to seyn no wers þan ȝe knowyn & ȝet not so euyl as ȝe knowyn. Neuyr-þe-lesse her ȝe seyn wers þan ȝe knowyn, God for-ȝeue it ȝow, for I am þat same persone to whom þes wordys ben arectyd, whech oftyntyme suffir gret schame & repref & am not gylty in þis mater, God I take to record." (244:34–245:3)

> ("Lo, sirs," she said. "You ought to say no worse than you know and yet not so evil as you know. Never the less here you say worse than you know, God forgive you, for I am that same person to whom these words are attributed, who often suffers great shame and reproof and am not guilty in this matter, as God is my witness.")

Yet as so often in *The Book of Margery Kempe* the significance of the episode in the book as a whole is rather more than Kempe's own reading of it and the obvious moral with which she rebukes the gathering. While the episode functions on one level to illustrate once more how little valued she is in the world of men and manners, it also illustrates her value in the eyes of God through suffering for him as Christ suffered for her. By describing her as the butt of gossip, the subject of a proverb, the story also carries a contradictory set of ideas that actually emphasises her importance. To be the force behind a proverb, a commonplace repeated far from the original events themselves, illustrates what is arguably a purpose of the *Book*, to demonstrate that Kempe is significant, talked about, and important. The episode suggests in a characteristically ambiguous fashion the tension between self-effacement and self-promotion that haunts the *Book* and the uneasy line that Kempe treads in the project of the *Book*. It also illustrates Kempe's keen awareness of the power of words and language, their ability to materially affect circumstances, and their status as sites of conflict within which battles for power can be fought. It is a moment in the text where Kempe finds herself textualised by her contemporaries and vigorously insists that her reality is not equivalent to its description by others. In other words Kempe insists that it is possible to distinguish between levels of reality and that some are significantly more truthful than others.

Over five centuries after Kempe's own times there are many different kinds of texts that describe themselves as in some way or another *The Book of Margery Kempe*, and there are many different kinds of contexts, many different ways, in which she has been textualised since that description in her own book. The history of our knowledge of the *Book* provides in some ways a history of the twentieth century itself, and the purpose of this book is to explore some of that history, to suggest how the *Book* has figured in the representation and understanding of the Middle Ages in the twentieth century.

One of the peculiarities of *The Book of Margery Kempe* is that it has only been known to scholars in its full form since 1934 but since then has seen a rapid growth in interest. As one of two manuscripts identified in that year, it is arguably also one of the last great medieval manuscript discoveries. In a sense *The Book of Margery Kempe* is a dark horse of the medieval world, coming from nowhere to generate wide-scale interest, particularly in comparison with the other medieval manuscript found in the same year, the Winchester Malory. In terms of Malory's work, there already were other manuscripts that had provided contexts and histories for scholarship and textual production, and, as David Matthews points out, *Morte D'Arthur* was already one of the better-known Middle English texts.[2] Eugene Vinaver was already working on a new edition when he read in *The Telegraph* of the manuscript discovery, and an Everyman edition with spelling modernized but otherwise a 'reprint of Caxton,'[3] was already in print. The appearance of the Kempe manuscript, on the other hand, was much more generally regarded as a literary event as the newspapers of the time record.[4] The nature of its existence had not been anticipated by scholars.

This book, then, is a book about *The Book of Margery Kempe*, tracing some of the ways in which it has appeared and been treated since its identification in the twentieth century and the ways in which it has come to speak of a particular period of time, the Middle Ages, or the medieval period in England. The modern formulations of the *Book* necessarily reflect not only to the fifteenth century but the twentieth and twenty-first centuries. While critics have speculated about the early readership of the manuscript of the full text,[5] the only forms in which anything about Kempe's text had come down to us previously from the medieval period were in the two editions of selections printed by Wynkyn de Worde in 1501 and Henry Pepwell in 1521. These selections, as Sue Ellen Holbrook has argued, focus on the devotional and exemplary passages from the text, designed to be used for the instruction of laywomen and religious counsellors alike.[6] In Worde's edition they stand alone; in Pepwell's, Kempe keeps company with Walter Hilton and Catherine of Siena, thus contributing to the initial positioning of Kempe as a mystic in spite of the fact that she is never so described in her own text. These were the contexts that shaped the sense of Kempe in the early twentieth century.

Until 1934 our understandings of Margery Kempe were primarily as a medieval mystic, a devout religious woman, the producer of *sententiae* of spiritual benefit. Undoubtedly part of the interest caused by the discovery of the full manuscript can be attributed to the fact that the previously known selections were revealed to be only the tip of the iceberg, with the remainder of the *Book* being much more varied and wide ranging in terms of material. The Salthouse manuscript contains not only religious devotion but also insights into the production and context of that devotion and the life of the person who experienced it.[7] The devotions have fuller human dimensions in the manuscript than could ever have been guessed from the extracts.

The Book of Margery Kempe is, as David Aers argues, 'one of the most fascinating English texts of the later Middle Ages, a precious work for anyone interested in the history of gender, subjectivities, and English culture.'[8] But the history of the *Book* in the twentieth and twenty-first centuries also resonates with the issues and concerns of that period so far from medieval England. The seventy years since its identification have seen the development and professionalisation of English Literature as a discipline, taught in schools, colleges and universities. They have also seen the secularisation of western cultures and, arguably, an ambiguous institutionalisation of some kind of feminism or at the least a sense that gender as a category is worth consideration on its own merits. The productions of *The Book of Margery Kempe* have been inflected by all of these changes.

From the very beginning of its publication history, *The Book of Margery Kempe*, as it came to be known, was unusual. The first production of the full text from the Salthouse manuscript was not a scholarly edition but a modernised edition;

the text was put into modern English and rearranged with the needs of a modern audience in mind in 1936 by Colonel Butler-Bowdon, the owner of the house in which the manuscipt was found. It was not until 1940 that a scholarly edition was produced by Sanford Brown Meech and Hope Emily Allen for the Early English Text Society. How it was that the owner of the manuscript came to be its first editor and that the identifier of the Salthouse manuscript, Hope Emily Allen, found herself marginalised from its first appearances in print are stories that are important to understandings of scholarship and literary production in the first decades of English literature as a discipline.[9]

A title page begins that story. 'The Book of Margery Kempe/Edited By/Sanford Brown Meech/With Prefatory Note By/Hope Emily Allen/And/Notes And Appendices/By/Sanford Brown Meech/And/Hope Emily Allen.' A formal announcement of authority and ownership. The acknowledgment of a text produced by different hands, separately identifying the contributions. And of course readers know that every story told is necessarily selective, carrying the traces of other stories not told, of other paths not taken. Each and every edition selects and presents its material according to some ideas and interests rather than others, consciously and unconsciously. But what emerges from a reading of this scholarly text, the only Middle English edition available for over fifty years, until 1996,[10] is the debate and dialogue between the editor and the supplier of the prefatory note. To read the text of Kempe's story in the EETS edition is to become aware of the other stories lurking and beckoning at the front and back of the book, surrounding the story that one goes to the book to read. Alerted by Allen's bold yet bland assertion at the beginning of the prefatory note, 'The notes supplied by me are signed,' we can then read for the differences in the extra-textual exegesis, to find another story running in counterpoint to Kempe's revelations. Meech's work, the default position, those notes not attended by the authoritative yet anxious mark of his collaborator's presence, 'H.E.A.,' are factual, historical, concerning issues of place, date and person. Allen's are more broadly contextual, speculative, referring ever outward and onward, both in allusions to the influence on Kempe of a Continental female mystical tradition and to the development of Allen's own work in a projected future volume. 'I shall,' she firmly states, 'discuss these points consecutively in the "synthesis of Margery, the mystic and the woman," to be given in my introduction in a later volume.'[11] 'Some of my notes look forward to my general introduction,' she repeats, 'to be given in a later volume,'[12] laying down a trail for researchers that thins, seventy years after these notes were written, when they find no such volume and comes to a halt at the shelves on which seven archival boxes of Allen's papers are patiently stacked in the library of Allen's alma mater, Bryn Mawr College, near Philadelphia. Here is an end, one residual fragment, of the voices that speak behind the pages of the sober and solid, brown and gold cover of the EETS edition of *The Book of Margery Kempe.*

What are the stories behind *The Book of Margery Kempe* in its modern incarnations? This book begins at the beginning of the history of the *Book*'s twentieth-century production and reception, explaining the contexts in which Hope Allen's identification of the manuscript and the first editions of the *Book* took place. In particular, it explores the rôle of Allen herself as an independent female scholar in the communities of scholarship from 1930 to her death in 1960, providing one example of how a medieval manuscript was re-produced and presented for both specialist and popular audiences. This aspect of the story is also indicative of changes in the nature of scholarship and the gender of those producing it. If the production of texts and commentaries about them had largely been a male preserve, an amateur and gentlemanly affair for groups such as the Roxburghe Club in the nineteenth century,[13] then the EETS and work by female scholars marked specific changes in the production of Middle English texts, expanding the range of people producing them, and the kinds of material it was thought appropriate to include in the commentaries. Once this context has been established, we can follow the public and scholarly debates that developed around the *Book*, from newspaper cuttings to academic discussions, within and outside the disciplines of English, History and Religion, within and beyond the notions of English as a national discourse. And again we can investigate a range of shapes and forms in which *The Book of Margery Kempe* has appeared in recent years, from spiritual guide to teaching text, to see what has been meant by and understood as *The Book of Margery Kempe*, watching the morphing and transmogrifications according to the needs and audiences of particular editions.

This kind of exploration of the making of the *The Book of Margery Kempe*, and the development of something that might be called Kempe studies, has been influenced and made possible by recent debates about what constitutes medieval studies. Historical contextualisations of the *Book*, specifically in relation to its reproductions in the twentieth century, are part of self-reflexive understandings of what medieval studies are and how they are undertaken. Paul Zumthor, for example, paints a picture of one kind of traditional understanding of what a medievalist did, of a practice where 'withdrawn into the bookish tranquillity of the study, one restored oneself in a slow, meticulous labor of establishing and classifying index cards whose effect was to remove the drama from life, death, and the destiny of men.'[14] Zumthor's work is part of a re-invigoration of medieval studies, in keeping with his observation in 1986 that 'many signs have appeared that proclaim a renewal of medieval studies, affecting both their procedures and the interest they arouse.'[15]

In producing alternative ways of thinking about the connections between twentieth-century scholars and medieval texts, Zumthor proposes four categories through which we might 'bring the ancient text into the present, that is…integrate it into that historicity which is ours.'[16] These four stages are the 'original communication,' the 'mediated communication I' that involves the production and reception of the manuscript, 'mediated communication II' that involves the scholar and the teaching context, and 'communication put in a form consumable today.' His suggestion is that we 'grasp, at each of the constituent phases in my scheme, the tradition of a textual practice, the complex act that produced an intention as well as a word, an inherent signifying effect, and a response.'[17]

Zumthor's scheme has many attractions. It suggests a real attempt to bring literature and history together and is both synchronic, looking at the manifestation of a text at one particular time, and diachronic, investigating changes through time. It also locates the text in concrete physical and material appearances, while including the realm of the cultural and ideological in considering the purposes to which the text is put. All of these issues are important to a text like *The Book of Margery Kempe* and its particular manifestations in the twentieth century and to an understanding of how the medieval period is re-made.

Other issues arise, however, in relation to one of the main areas in which the *Book* has attracted attention—gender studies. From 1934 onwards, part of the significance of the *Book* was always seen to be the fact that its originator was a woman. Debates arose as to the level of agency one could ascribe to Kempe for the *Book*, given that she was at some levels 'illiterate' and dictated the work to scribes. Her rôle as author of the text is ambiguous, but the sense of the singularity of the text has always partly involved the gender of its 'author.' The identification of the Salthouse manuscript then coincided with the development of interest in issues relating to gender and with the increase in numbers of women as readers, as teachers, as scholars. More recently *The Book of Margery Kempe* has attracted interest from critics outside medieval studies partly because of a broadening in the scope of literary feminism. For many years it had been argued that the proper objects of study for feminist literary scholarship were the immediate past and the present, the late nineteenth century and the twentieth century. What happened before the self-conscious awareness of women's rights and struggles for social and economic equality was of relatively little interest for contemporary feminists. In the last twenty years feminist scholars have turned their attention to earlier women writers, to the seventeenth century, to the Renaissance, and to the medieval period. In doing so they have brought forward little-known women writers, and texts significant for their discussion of gender issues. In this way the literary 'tradition' has been re-evaluated, and the notion of an all-male canon of great writers has been challenged significantly. *The Book of Margery Kempe* has played a part in that re-evaluation, often being cited as an example of the earliest writing by women.

Yet in rediscovering women's history there has been a tendency, as writers such as Sheila Delany and Elizabeth Fox-Genovese have argued, to appropriate women from distant historical periods and to consider them through modern feminist theories at the expense of their own historically specific contexts.[18] In relation to *The Book of Margery Kempe*, for example, the tendency to psychologise the woman on the basis of the text can be seen in the modernised version of the *Book* by Louise Collis and in some work by critics.[19] Indeed, while Karma Lochrie's scholarly and insightful book *Margery Kempe and Translations of the Flesh*[20] contributes much to a re-thinking of the *Book* and the person, there is nevertheless a tendency to find subversion everywhere subversive, transgressions rather than conformity, which reflects twentieth-century values rather more than fifteenth-century values. Given the paucity of information about Margery Kempe outside of the *Book*, there is also a tendency to take her at the *Book*'s word, which, as Sue Ellen Holbrook rightly identifies, provides dangers of its own and fails to acknowledge the constructedness of the text, its status 'as a treatise with theological content.'[21]

The Book of Margery Kempe, put simply, as some critics from Hope Allen in the 1930s to those of today have recognised, has an orthodox and devout intention that cannot be gainsaid by modern criticism. One suggestion that this book has to make is that feminism might play a broader rôle in thinking about *The Book of Margery Kempe* than focussing only on Kempe herself. A more broadly conceived and materialist feminist practice might not only look for historical texts produced by women but might include within its remit an analysis of the kinds of scholarship that have arisen around *The Book of Margery Kempe* as well as the text itself, beginning with the identifier of the Salthouse manuscript, Hope Allen, and her colleagues, recognising both the individual work as well as the collective contexts in which it was produced.

The contribution of feminism to a re-evaluation of history and literature that re-focusses critical attention has often been remarked and has been crucial in not only expanding the range of topics under consideration but also in ways of reconsidering those topics. Nowhere is this clearer than in medieval studies, which exerted a fascination for, and was open to, women scholars in ways and for reasons which are only now being discussed in any detail.[22] Yet the paths of feminism through discussions of history have been divergent, calling into question how feminism is being defined. The astute insights of Sheila Delany, in this context, demonstrate the inappropriateness of regarding women such as Christine de Pizan as feminist simply because of their gender, and the need to include accounts of class and politics,[23] rather than simply mine history for examples of remarkable women, secure in their isolation.[24]

In thinking about textual production, about how the *Book* has been made and re-made, another contribution to medieval studies can also be made by adopting an approach more frequently applied to the Renaissance—cultural materialism. As a label, 'cultural materialism' has been variously used in the past thirty years but, following its application to the Renaissance, is being increasingly applied to other historical periods, in a variety of ways. At one end of the scale it has been used simply to express the assumption that culture has a material dimension; at the other, critics have wanted to insist on its specific political principles.[25] Given this, it is important to address what the term has meant and how it might add to Zumthor's program of approach to medieval texts such as *The Book of Margery Kempe*.

In *Cultural Materialism: The Struggle for a Science of Culture* (1979), Marvin Harris, on the basis of having used the phrase in 1968, claimed to be its originator: 'I did not invent "cultural materialism," I am responsible for giving it its name (in *The Rise of Anthropological Theory*).'[26] For Harris, an anthropologist, cultural materialism was fundamentally scientific in character:

> Cultural materialism shares with other scientific strategies an epistemology which seeks to restrict fields of inquiry to events, entities, and relationships that are knowable by means of explicit, logico-empirical, inductive-deductive, quantifiable public procedures or 'operations' subject to replication by independent observers.[27]

Current users of the term do not generally appeal to cultural materialism as a 'scientific strategy' and would probably want to argue that science needs to be scrutinised for its own imbrication with culture rather than be presumed outside it. Harris' use does, however, highlight cultural materialism's insistence on the materiality of culture in the sense that a cultural artefact can be analysed in terms of 'relationships that are knowable.' Literary cultural materialism, in this sense, is partly reacting against approaches to literature that emphasised personal empathy between reader and author, seen less as a matter of analysis than intuition.

Principally, the notion that culture must be seen as material stands in opposition to the Romantic idea that culture, or literature, is ideal, existing outside social, political and economic structures. The text is not seen as intuitively created by a single God-like author, rather amusingly caricatured by the Russian critic and poet Vladimir Mayakovsky in 1926, who criticised the idea that 'the only method of production is the inspired throwing back of the head while one waits for the heavenly soul of poetry to descend on one's bald patch in the form of a dove, a peacock or an ostrich.'[28]

More recently, in the debates of the last decade, cultural materialism struggles against the worst excesses of 'our present cultural situation,' as Lee Patterson puts it, 'let us follow current practice and call it postmodernism.'[29] In this context the emphasis on relationships that are knowable includes an insistence that it is possible to make statements about culture and cultural works that have meaning and that some statements have more validity or significance than others. Here cultural materialism argues that there is a materiality and reality beyond the language through which knowledge of that materiality is inevitably expressed and constructed.

Here cultural materialism diverges from Zumthor's scheme in its understanding of the importance of a concept of materiality. For Zumthor,

> [o]ur discourse contains three levels of reality, each one as fleeting and uncertain as the others: that of the events (for us, the medieval texts), that of history as such, and that of the text that we are writing. The first creates the third, which interprets the second, which makes the first perceptible.[30]

While the schema as initially outlined seems to connect production with communication and reception in ways that acknowledge differences between those procedures, this formulation collapses those differences. In this statement the medieval text inspires the scholarly text through which history is interpreted. Each of these levels is as 'fleeting and uncertain' as the others, which brings us back to a version of textualism where nothing has more validity and certainty than anything else. If this were not enough, we need to remember the framing first sentence that tells us that these 'three levels of reality' are contained, that is occur, within, our 'discourse.' If textuality is labyrinthine,[31] then so is discourse, thus conceived, and we appear to be back in the maze of language from which there is no escape, in which Margery Kempe describes herself as being falsely imprisoned and from which the Salthouse manuscript was her designated line of escape.

Books on shelves and desks, in libraries personal and institutional, in bookshops and in homes, necessarily make statements about what kind of thing they are, who their audience is and what might be done with them. The hardcover Middle English edition labouriously produced by Meech and Allen for the EETS solidly survives the attentions of the specialist student, asserting its resilience through time. The first paperback Penguin modernisation, with its colourful cover, engages the attention of a more diverse audience, those in search of women in history, of spiritual guidance, of the eccentricities of English literature, eventually falling apart in a form designed for a more transient passage through history. Quite different materialities are manifested in these productions.

Quite different, too, are the cultural materialities behind these physical productions of the text. The notion that scholarship might exist in some ethereal and objective world, unaffected by material circumstances disintegrates when we piece together the stories of the early work on Kempe's text. These productions then turn out to be affected by political, economic and social factors, arguments about literature and culture, understandings about gender, not only in the fifteenth century but in the twenty-first century too. Thinking about Allen not only as a scholar but as a female scholar in terms of her difficult involvement with the Kempe text alerts us to the ways in which some things relating to gender and cultural production change and some stay the same. These kinds of circumstances, these zones of influence, on the textual commodity profoundly affect the form and shape of texts and the influence that the text itself might come to have.

Cultural materialism, begun by Harris, developed by the British marxist Raymond Williams,[32] in debate with the American approaches of New Historicism combines 'historical context, theoretical method, political commitment and textual analysis' and 'studies the implications of literary texts in history.'[33] What is important here is thinking not only about texts but about scholarship itself as having constitutive rôles in social organisations[34] as influential in broader contexts than simply the production of another book to be bought or borrowed, and read. Scholarship itself is embedded in social relations and tells us about the different kinds of cultures from which it comes, and attests to its own status as a 'practical social activity.'[35] Cultural materialism can help us see books and writing, the production of history itself, not as so many 'dead object[s] to be marvelled at'[36] but as processes that help to shed light on our own contemporary practices of cultural production.

In particular, these principles help to inform a re-examination of what it is that we mean when we refer to *The Book of Margery Kempe*. The different forms and shapes in which the book appears obviously influence the experience and practice of reading the text. In turn, the circulation of the *Book* in its various shapes influences how the Middle Ages are seen as in some ways Kempe and her book take on exemplary status. And again, knowledge of Kempe contributes to various kinds of understandings of what English literature is and has been as well as to understandings of Englishness and England itself. At various stages in the history of the *Book* we can see how scholarship and criticism about it are part of broader patterns and cultural meanings. Cultural materialism then provides a framework for thinking about how *The Book of Margery Kempe* has been produced, re-produced and disseminated, how it has been made and re-made.

Let's have a look at some of the stories behind the story that we think of as *The Book of Margery Kempe* in its various forms and see where its history in the twentieth century began, holding onto the index cards, as Zumthor put it, resolutely refusing to remove the drama from life, and acknowledging the different kinds of materialities from which these stories came, and to which they gave rise.[37]

Notes

1. Sanford Brown Meech & Hope Emily Allen, *The Book of Margery Kempe* (London: The Early English Text Society, 1940), p. 244:6. All future references to the text will be included in brackets, giving page and line references.
2. David Matthews, *The Making of Middle English: 1765–1910* (Minneapolis: The University of Minnesota Press, 1999), pp. 92–3.
3. W. F. Oakeshott, 'The Finding of the Manuscript,' *Essays on Malory*, ed. J. A. Bennett, (Oxford: Clarendon, 1963), p. 4.
4. Chapter 4 has a discussion of these records.
5. Hope Emily Allen suggests in her unpublished notes that there might have been an audience amongst whom the manuscript circulated (Bryn Mawr College Archives). Sue Ellen Holbrook also suggests that the selections from the *Book* published by Wynkyn de Worde can be seen as '[a]nother testimonial to the reception' of the *Book*, '"About Her": Margery Kempe's Book of Feeling and Working,' *The Idea of Medieval Literature: New Essays on Chaucer and Medieval Culture in Honor of Donald R. Howard*, ed. James M. Dean and Christian K. Zacher (Newark: University of Delaware Press, 1992), p. 278.
6. Ibid..
7. The Salthouse manuscript is named after the scribe of the only extant copy who wrote 'Ihesu mercy quod salthows' at the end of the text. See EETS p. xxxiii.
8. David Aers, *Community, Gender, and Individual Identity: English Writing 1360–1430* (London: Routledge, 1988), p.74.
9. John C. Hirsh first began this story in his biography, *Hope Emily Allen: Medieval Scholarship and Feminism* (Norman, Oklahoma: Pilgrim Books, 1988).

10. In that year, 1996, *The Book of Margery Kempe*, edited by Lynn Staley for TEAMS, Kalamazoo, Michigan, Medieval Institute Publications, was published.

11. Sanford Brown Meech and Hope Emily Allen, 1940, p. lvii.

12. Ibid., p. 255.

13. See David Matthews, *The Making of Middle English*, chapter 4.

14. Paul Zumthor, *Speaking of the Middle Ages*, tr. Sarah White (Lincoln: University of Nebraska Press, 1986), p. 49.

15. Ibid., p. 8. Description of a 'new medievalism' is also important here. See, for example, R. Howard Bloch and Stephen Nichols, *Medievalism and the Modernist Temper* (Baltimore: The Johns Hopkins University Press, 1996); Marina S. Brownlee, Kevin Brownlee and Stephen G. Nichols, *The New Medievalism* (Baltimore: The Johns Hopkins University Press, 1991).

16. Ibid., p. 33.

17. Ibid., p. 26.

18. Sheila Delany, '"Mothers to Think back through": Who Are They? The Ambiguous Example of Christine de Pizan,' in Laurie A. Finke and Martin B. Shichtman, eds., *Medieval Texts and Contemporary Readers* (Ithaca: Cornell University Press, 1987), pp.177–192, and, for a more general discussion of 'The Struggle for a Feminist History,' see Elizabeth Fox-Genovese, *Feminism Without Illusions: A Critique of Individualism* (Chapel Hill: The University of North Carolina Press, 1991), especially chapter 6.

19. Louise Collis, *The Apprentice Saint* (London: Michael Joseph, 1964). See, for example, Nancy F. Partner's psychoanalytic approach in 'Reading *The Book of Margery Kempe*,' *Exemplaria* 3,1 March 1991, pp. 29-66, and '"And Most of All for Inordinate Love": Desire and Denial in *The Book of Margery Kempe*,' *Thought*, vol. 64, No. 254 (September 1989), pp. 254–267.

20. Karma Lochrie, *Margery Kempe and Translations of the Flesh* (Philadelphia: University of Pennsylvania Press, 1991).

21. Sue Ellen Holbrook, '"About Her,"' p. 266.

22. Maxine Berg's *A Woman in History: Eileen Power 1889–1940* (Cambridge: Cambridge University Press, 1996), and John C. Hirsh's *Hope Emily Allen: Medieval Scholarship and Feminism* (Norman, Oklahoma: Pilgrim, 1988) are excellent contributions to a cultural materialist history which includes the neglected work of women without abstracting them from their contexts or reifying them. In this respect, Edward Shils & Carmen Becker's *Cambridge Women: Twelve Portraits* (Cambridge: Cambridge University Press, 1996) has a different emphasis and is rather a celebration of the institution of Cambridge University than an evaluation of women scholars in a fuller context. See also Bonnie G. Smith, 'The Contribution of Women to Modern Historiography in Great Britain, France, and the United States, 1750–1940,' *The American Historical Review*, 89, June 1984, pp. 709–732, and Margaret Hastings and Elizabeth G. Kimball, 'Two Distinguished Medievalists: Nellie Neilson and Bertha Puttnam,' *The Journal of British Studies*, XVIII.2: pp. 142–59.

23. Sheila Delany, 1987.

24. In this context, the work of Sarah Beckwith, Sue Ellen Holbrook and others provides a significant contribution to analysis which is both feminist and materialist.

25. In February 1999 the Arizona Centre for Medieval and Renaissance Studies hosted a conference titled 'Material Culture and Cultural Materialisms in the Middle Ages and the Renaissance' which played on some of these differences. Critics have also examined the

differences between various approaches in their understandings of what materiality means. See, for example, Gabrielle M. Spiegel, 'History, Historicism, and the Social Logic of the Text in the Middle Ages,' *Speculum*, 65 1990, which argues that New Historicism, in particular, has problems in this context: 'Thus, what may have begun as an attempt to rescue literature from its privileged being and New Critical self-enclosure has paradoxically extended the boundaries of the literary to include social and material reality, thereby dissolving the material into "meaning"'(p. 69).

26. Marvin Harris, *Cultural Materialism: The Struggle for a Science of Culture* (New York: Random House, 1979), p. x.

27. Ibid., p. 27.

28. Vladimir Mayakovsky, *How Are Verses Made?* tr. G. M. Hyde (London: Jonathan Cape, 1974), p. 12.

29. Lee Patterson, ed. *Literary Practice and Social Change in Britain 1380-1530* (Berkeley: University of California Press, 1990), p. 87.

30. Ibid., p. 88.

31. Gabrielle M. Spiegel, 1990, p. 73.

32. See, in particular, Raymond Williams, *Marxism and Literature* (Oxford: Oxford University Press, 1977), pp. 5–6, and Raymond Williams, *The Long Revolution* (Harmondsworth: Penguin, 1965), p. 61. For a good overview of the historical development of cultural materialism, see Andrew Milner, *Cultural Materialism* (Melbourne: Melbourne University Press, 1993). The clearest and most rigorous attempt to identify the core issues of cultural materialism as a marxist practice can be found in H. Gustav Klaus, 'Cultural Materialism: A Summary of Principles,' eds. W. John Morgan & Peter Preston, *Raymond Williams: Politics, Education and Letters* (London: St Martin's Press, 1993), 88-104.

33. Jonathan Dollimore and Alan Sinfield, *Political Shakespeare: New Essays in Cultural Materialism* (Manchester: Manchester University Press, 1985), vii & viii.

34. H. Gustav Klaus, 1993, pp. 89–90.

35. Ibid., p. 49.

36. Ibid., p. 97.

37. Paul Zumthor, 1986, p. 49.

✠ Chapter 2

'Watchdogs on the Field':
Hope Allen and *The Book of Margery Kempe*

In March 1949, after the event, Hope Allen attributed the happy accident of being called on to identify the manuscript of Margery Kempe to the inability of some scholars to escape from preconceptions and received opinions. She wrote to the Early English Text Society secretary, Mabel Day, that her luck in being the person on the scene reinforced her belief in the necessity of clearing 'our minds of all preconceptions or we will miss clues to great discoveries (those who were first approached as to the Butler-Bowdon MS did not go to see it, being so sure the BMK was written by an anchoress).'[1] How, then, did Allen happen to be the person to whom identification of the manuscript fell, and how did this contribute to the modern history of *The Book of Margery Kempe*?

John C. Hirsh's important biography of Allen[2] provides a full account of her life from 1883–1960 and her career and is a significant contribution to a cultural materialist account of the scholarship of this period. Here I deal only with Allen's relationship with *The Book of Margery Kempe* in the context of her social and intellectual life as a way of identifying the beginnings of what was to become what might now be called Kempe studies. Analyses of her work on the book, the intellectual and personal foundations of her approach, and the community of scholars in which she worked—the subject of the following chapter—then provide a basis for building a picture of scholarship outside tertiary institutions in the middle of the last century. This is a picture to put alongside those of scholars and women scholars in particular—on whom less work has been done than on their male counterparts—within institutions of higher education and research.

That the Kempe manuscript should fall into the hands of Allen was at once both serendipitous and symptomatic, an intriguing example of the felicities and travails of scholarship. As Hirsh argues, Allen's reputation as a scholar was founded on her articles on *Ancren Riwle*, the thirteenth-century spiritual guide, and cemented by the 1931 publication of *The English Writings of Richard Rolle Hermit of Hampole* for Oxford University Press.[3] From as early as 1910, American-born Allen visited England for various stints of research and became known to English scholars in the field so that by 1934 Allen 'was a recognized authority in Britain as well as in America, in the field of medieval English mystical and devotional manuscripts.'[4] When Colonel Butler-Bowdon then took his manuscript to the Victoria and Albert Museum,[5] Evelyn Underhill, also working on medieval mysticism, suggested that her cousin, Allen, back in London at this point in June 1934, would be the most appropriate person to assess the material.[6]

The clearest sense of Allen's work on the *Book* arises from archival material, her notes and letters[7]—material in which she describes to others and for herself what she is trying to achieve and how she intends to go about it. The best accounts survive in letters to scholars with whom she felt she had most in common. By definition, of course, when she was with these people, as she was in the middle of 1934, she had no need to write to them to explain. It is quite frustrating in that sense to have no report in Allen's own words of how identifying the manuscript must have felt. All that seems to remain is a brief postcard to Dorothy Ellis, a scholar from Newnham College, Cambridge,[8] on 23 August 1934 on which she declares 'The MS at S.Ken.[sington][9] is too thrilling for words.'[10] Otherwise, evidence of the difficulties that developed surrounding the preparation of the material for the Early English Text Society's (EETS) edition overshadows the delight Allen must initially have felt though one shrewd reviewer did manage to detect something from the EETS volume, objective and scholarly as it appeared, when it was published in 1940:

> there is little hint of the excitement Miss Allen must have felt when she examined Colonel Butler-Bowdon's discovery—unless it is in the almost pent-up manner in which she tells us what she hopes to give in Volume 2.[11]

There is substantial evidence within the archival collections to support the reviewer's intuition, as Hirsh documents, and it is necessary to turn back to Allen's own intellectual and family history to understand why her work on Kempe was, as she saw it, both the best and the worst project she could have undertaken and to understand how some of the traditions that developed in Kempe studies were established. Through this kind of investigation we can get closer to seeing the constitution of the particular kind of scholarship into which *The Book of Margery Kempe* was born and the rôle of a particular woman in that constitution.

Hirsh's account of Allen's rôle in the production of the *Book* is very revealing. He illustrates, from the manuscripts, letters and archival material, just how fraught was the production of the scholarly artefact EETS 212. In the first telling of the tale of Allen's marginalisation from what was originally her project, Hirsh rightly emphasised the frustration and displeasure Allen felt as a result of her deteriorating relationships with Colonel Butler-Bowdon and Sanford Brown Meech, a young Ph.D. scholar whom she had asked to work on the edition. Reading through the archival material one can, however, put together an analysis which does not so much contradict Hirsh's interpretation as add to an explanation of how Allen came to be in a very difficult position. An exploration of the background of the independent scholar demonstrates that she can be seen less as a victim than as a person whose own complex history contributed to the peculiarly stressful and unpleasant academic collaboration that was *The Book of Margery Kempe*.[12] This approach sheds light not only on the completed *Book* but also provides some reasons why the projected second volume was never finished.

Born on November 12, 1883, Hope Emily Allen was not directly a child of the experimental communitarian society at Oneida, New York, in which her parents spent some time. Unlike her brother Grosvenor Noyes, Allen was born after her parents left the community, but she retained a lifelong interest in its progress and history. Now part of the story of American communitarian societies of the eighteenth and nineteenth centuries, Oneida is seen as one of those experiments in stirpiculture, or eugenics, which attempted to combine religious and communistic values. Established in 1847 by John Humphrey Noyes, after whom Allen's brother was named, the group rejected marriage on the grounds that it treated women like property. Noyes himself, writing about Oneida in the *History of American Socialisms* (1869), described the community through the two central books produced by the community, *The Berean* (1847) and *Bible Communism* (1848).

Drawing on the Bible, Noyes argued against contemporary social values which, a marxist might now put it, commodified women:

> [W]e affirm that there is no intrinsic difference between property in persons and property in things; and that the same spirit which abolished exclusiveness in regard to money, would abolish, if circumstances allowed full scope to it, exclusiveness in regard to women and children. Paul expressly places property in women and property in goods in the same category, and speaks of them together, as ready to be abolished by the advent of the Kingdom of Heaven. "The time," says he, "is short; it remaineth that they that have wives be as though they had none; and they that buy as though they possessed not; for the fashion of this world passeth away." 1 Cor. 7:29–31.

> The abolishment of appropriation is involved in the very nature of a true relation to
> Christ in the gospel.[13]

Going on to argue from grammar that 'I' and 'mine' and the 'possessive feeling' that they represent relate back to egotism, Noyes states:

> The grand distinction between the Christian and the unbeliever, between heaven and the
> world, is, that in one reigns the We-spirit, and in the other the I-spirit. From *I* comes *mine*,
> and from the I-spirit comes exclusive appropriation of money, women, etc. From *we* comes
> *ours*, and from the We-spirit comes universal community of interests.[14]

This account gives one example of the ways in which the believers in this community were re-evaluating the rôles of women. Here women were not mere decorative toys, testaments to their husbands' wealth and worldly status. Nor were women to be determined solely by their reproductive capacities. Indeed child-bearing was not to be regarded as a matter of individual choice where the child became a possessed object, symbolic of the relationship between two adults. Nor should these theories be taken as sanctioning licentiousness, argued the community.

> Free love with us does *not* mean freedom to love to-day and leave to-morrow; nor freedom
> to take a woman's person and keep our property to ourselves; nor freedom to freight a
> woman with our offspring and send her down stream without care or help; nor freedom to
> beget children and leave them on the street and the poor-house.[15]

Clearly the extent to which these statements translated to any improved conditions for women depended entirely on how well they were carried out. It is also clear that the arguments retain a male orientation. The addressee is hypothesised as male; the 'freighting' and 'begetting' are obviously done by the men, yet on paper at least there is an egalitarianism in the Oneida community at odds with many other aspects of nineteenth-century America. There seems to have been no division of labour and a direct rejection of the contemporary 'separate spheres' ideology that saw women in the home and men outside. In this context, Hirsh writes that on the birth of Allen's brother, her parents Portia Underhill (distant cousin of medievalist Evelyn Underhill) and Henry C. Allen were apparently ordered to separate because they demonstrated an unacceptably exclusive relationship. When the community broke up, they married, and Hope Allen was born under more conventional circumstances.

From the outset of the Second World War in 1939 until her death in 1960 Allen was based in Oneida, at Kenwood, New York. Although the community had changed in Allen's lifetime, being now more business corporation than religious community, it maintained some aspects of the shared living arrangements that had been an intrinsic part of its origins. From Allen's letters her continued interest in the community is clear. She sent histories of the community to friends and scholars who she thought might be interested. In a letter to C. T. Onions in about 1947 she described 'the very peculiar and exceptional home which at once gives me remarkable security and ease of living (unusual for a woman scholar), and on the other of course does to some degree slow down my progress.' In doing so she often pointed out her own rooms in the 'two top floors of the squaretower with the flag[pole].'[16] In this sense Allen enjoyed what Virginia Woolf described in 1928 as the absolute necessity of 'a room of one's own' and financial independence, both of which in different ways were provided by the Oneida communities.[17] That Allen's long-time friend Joan Wake, at least, had read Woolf's book is evident in a letter she sent to Allen.[18] Wake regarded the book as 'Too self-conscious and dramatic, but quite excellent in parts,' and her interest is as one might have expected of a book that explicitly deals with the position of women in relation to education, learning, and the creation of literature. Allen had the physical, emotional and psychological space that Woolf argues are essential requirements for creative activity. Where *A Room of One's Own* seems to suggest that personal space and financial independence are the main requirements for independent thought and creative energy, Allen was rather more aware that one nevertheless lives in a houseful of others, in society in one form or another. Allen's particular sense of community is recognised in the obligations that this visited upon her. Furthermore, the Oneida Community's re-evaluation of the rôles of women provided a significant contribution to Allen's intellectual development and her abiding interest in women's history and circumstances.

In a letter fragment, annotated and dated by Joan Wake as 'part of unfinished letter to Mabel Day—dated 18 Aug 1952,' Allen describes how after the collapse of the Oneida Community, she was still brought up within the remnants of its framework.

> The accident of having developed industries gave a joint-stock company in which the old members owned the stock, and thus they were unexpectedly kept together after the 'break-up', and lived together in rented family apartments in the community house (in this small settlement there was no other place to live). So I was born among them, some years after the resumption of worldly life, of parents who had their only other child in the community.[19]

In various letters Allen described how the Oneida community and its history had directly and indirectly influenced her development. In a letter dated January 29, 1943, Allen referred to Ray Strachey's *Religious Fanaticism* as containing 'an essay on this place which gives the best external account.' She continued to explain her own adult interests in relation to childhood influences:

> [M]y mother's reminiscences started my interest in religious psychology and the family isolation from their relatives 'outside' made me sympathise with the medieval ideal of martyrdom (as did the hardships of the discipline here). Since half of our family on each side was Episcopalian I was better prepared for medieval studies than most of the Puritan-descended majority of my 'clan'.[20]

In a further letter a few years later, on March 12, 1949, Allen again wrote of her family influences, of the way her grandmother 'directed my thoughts to the past from an early age.'

> My mother—who joined the Oneida Community, that most eccentric religious society, with friends and was cast off by her family for so doing—talked to me as much on religious history as my grandmother Allen on revolutionary....The/my family background altogether...makes me tolerate the sort of religious history which most persons of my state of Christian agnosticism would hate.[21]

While Allen was not naïve about the success of the community, neither was she disrespectful of its aims, describing it as seeming 'to her the most intense and comprehensive experiment in human behaviour ever made.'[22] She stated firmly 'I (and I believe most of the descendants of the community) retain the greatest respect for our communistic ancestors.' Yet in a letter, which on internal evidence from a reference to 'your *Man and Superman*' seems addressed to George Bernard Shaw, she certainly denied that it could be seen as a model for any socialist utopia.[23]

> In any case it could never be repeated without the condition of strong leadership, and a resultant strong organisation, of theological conviction and isolation from the world which gave it its peculiar stability. Anyone who borrowed its license without its discipline would be violating the essential spirit of the institution.[24]

One other aspect of the original Oneida community bears some description here for its possible impact on Allen's scholarly attitudes. In 1946 she wrote, 'The life of the community was based on a rigorous system of "Mutual Criticism"—very psychologically administered and heroically received—which drove away the pleasure seekers.'[25] In a quasi-anthropological study first published in 1875, *The Communistic Societies of the United States*, Charles Nordhoff describes his visit to Oneida and his observations of these people who were also called 'the perfectionists.' Noyes' 'system of mutual criticism' Nordhoff saw as 'a most important and ingenious device'[26] designed to teach mutual and self-correction, subdue the ego, and scourge pride and vanity. In place of inordinate love of the self were to be mutual respect and self-criticism.

Nordhoff describes in some detail one particular encounter he witnessed where a young man, called 'Charles' by the author for the sake of convenience, one Sunday afternoon 'offered himself for criticism.' When asked by Noyes what he wished to say about himself, 'Charles' offered up intellectual problems from which he saw himself as suffering, including 'being drawn away from God.'[27] The range of criticism which then came from the group of fifteen included a wide variety of personal faults such as being 'haughty and supercilious,' being 'a respecter of persons' and being overly critical about food at the table. Nordhoff's account provides a picture of that half-hour interview that is harrowing for those of us brought up in less forthright circumstances.

> Amid all this very plain speaking…Charles sat speechless, looking before him; but as the accusations multiplied, his face grew paler, and drops of perspiration began to stand on his forehead.[28]

At the end, as Nordhoff reports it, Noyes himself took over and provided consoling and supportive remarks about the work and effort Charles had recently displayed in self-correction, specifically in separating himself from 'an exclusive intimacy with the woman who was to bear a child through him.'[29]

Evidence for a similar kind of plain speaking can sometimes be seen in Allen's work and letters. The Allen archives contain many sustained correspondences between Allen and scholars working on medieval texts around the world. One such correspondence illustrates Allen's tendency for plain speaking and the way it was received. Sister Anna Maria of St Joseph's College, Bradford, in England, began writing to Allen whilst doing her thesis on Julian of Norwich. Allen's typical generosity is evident in the sister's thanks for the gift of airmail paper Allen had sent her. This, in turn, led to the nun's statement that she might not always use airmail, though if the matter were urgent she would.

> Otherwise I shall write by ordinary mail, as being more in accord with the vow of Poverty that I have made. I do hope you will forgive my being so candid about this—but I think you understand our life well enough to appreciate the fact that I have to be a good nun even before being a good student, though I trust I shall succeed in being both! (BMC)

To such a open explanation Allen replies with corresponding frankness which, in its demands for scholarly rigour, is less than sensitive to the nun's religious position. Allen begins her letter by explaining that she uses airmail to save time. By 1949 Allen was very much aware of how much remained to be done on her scholarly work, how little there was to show for her endeavours. 'I send by air because I have so many obligations of various sorts that it helps to get off any one when it is on my mind, and saves precious time by not having to get back into it after I have begun on something else.' From this specific response to her correspondent, Allen launches into a series of reflections concerning religious scholarship not designed to make Sister Anna Maria sanguine about her likelihood of success.

> I am glad to think that a nun can be a good scholar as well as a good nun, but I have enough experience of various orders medieval and modern to know that interpretations differ greatly. I am glad to say that of the many Catholics—almost all of them religious—with whom I have been associated in scholarship those who fell behind what I feel to be due to scholarship (perhaps in part from a morbid zeal of some sort) were in the end corrected by co-religionists publicly, so that I had no embarrassment as a non-Catholic in the matter…scholarly pursuits require ideals which may clash with narrow workings of monastic. If you too much hamper your equipment because of the vow of poverty your work will be inaccurate and the reputation of conventional learning will suffer and the best scholars Catholic and others will not feel they can entrust important work to nuns. (BMC)

Trenchant as Allen's criticism is here and elsewhere, as spectacularly as it marks her, unlike the hapless 'Charles,' as no regarder of persons, it is criticism taken kindly for its intent. In July 1952 Sister Anna Maria wrote to Allen that 'only *I* know how badly needed and how efficacious your sometimes harsh but always well-meant comments have been.' (BMC)

If some of the Oneida values can be argued to have made Allen the committed, generous, forthright scholar she was, another major series of influences must have been those she encountered at Bryn Mawr College, Pennsylvania. Allen explains in a fragment of a letter to Mabel Day in 1952 that whereas it took half of her father's salary to send her brother Grosvenor to Yale, financial considerations were even more of an issue when it was decided that Allen should go to Bryn Mawr in 1902. It appears that Allen herself was reluctant to make the move, but that her brother, 'really a 4th parent to me, and the final directing force for my studies and life for years,'[30] helped to persuade her.

As Hirsh argued, the seriousness with which Bryn Mawr College treated scholarship and study by women 'would have been congenial to a disposition formed in part by the selective and rigorous requirements of Oneida.'[31] It was the expectation of Bryn Mawr College that women should study and achieve. While now the College takes some male students and operates in a very different way than it did in the early part of the twentieth century, it is still striking how congenial the atmosphere is for those women privileged enough to be there. How much more unusual this must have been in the days when there were still debates as to whether education was a suitable endeavour for women. Bryn Mawr

College's active engagement in these debates can be seen in the participation of the College President during Allen's time there, M. Carey Thomas. In 1899 Thomas explicitly attacked arguments that women's education should be organised on quite different grounds to men's. Her anger was particularly provoked by a speech by Charles W. Eliot, president of Harvard, as she wrote to a friend.

> Eliot disgraced himself. He said the traditions of past learning and scholarship were of no use to women's education, that women's words were as unlike men's as their bodies, that women's colleges ought to be schools of *manners* and really was hateful.[32]

Ardent advocate of equality in women's education, if need be in separate women's colleges until society sufficiently revalued women's rôles for them not to be subordinated within co-educational structures, Thomas reiterated her arguments in 1901, the year before Allen arrived. Given that knowledge itself does not change according to the nature of the knower, that there are material realities, why should the gender of the knowledge seeker or applier render that knowledge different?

> There is no reason to believe that typhoid or scarlet fever or phthisis can be successsfully treated by a woman physician in one way and by a male physician in another way. There is indeed every reason to believe that unless treated in the best way, the patient may die, the sex of the doctor affecting the result even less than the sex of the patient...the objects of competition are one and the same for both men and women—instructorships and professors' chairs, scholarly fame, and power to advance, however little, the outposts of knowledge.[33]

Allen graduated from the class of 1905 with a broad liberal arts degree, and her adult work can be seen to have been influenced by strands from her immediate family background, from the more diffuse ambience of Oneida, and from the expectations and skills encouraged at Bryn Mawr College. Allen's unconventional upbringing contributed to her breadth of understanding and ability to look beyond the obvious.

Given Allen's background and intellectual training at Bryn Mawr College it is not surprising that her methodology as a medievalist should be inclusive and broad ranging. Medieval studies perhaps inherently encourages interdisciplinary work,[34] and to some extent Allen's refusal to compartmentalise or to separate one field of investigation from another became one of the sources of tension between herself and Meech in relation to *The Book of Margery Kempe*. It is also possible to characterise these differences as part of a shift in expectations about what producing an edition meant, Allen's approach being part of a broader, more speculative style, facilitated by the EETS, beginning with its foundation in 1864 by Frederick Furnivall.[35] Understandably, particularly from a twenty-first century perspective, she seemed to find it difficult to separate issues of mysticism from secular concerns in her work on Kempe and resented being circumscribed in her research.

In notes for her work on *Ancrene Riwle* Allen wrote of the need for a 'history of culture,' of the need to work beyond disciplinary borders and to do more than write histories of establishments. In this sense her work is critical of what has since been described as history from the top down:

> my work would combine literary and historical research and concentrate on what would interpret religion as it was brought home to the individual, rather than as it touched ecclesiastical institutions or theological doctrines. (BMC)

Allen's work is part of a move away from the purely philological, language-based, approach to medieval studies that had been the dominant paradigm without sacrificing the accuracy and exactness encouraged by these emphases. While very much concerned with issues of language and etymology, as her work on the *Middle English Dictionary* and her published and unpublished material indicate, she nevertheless also demonstrated a concern with culture in the sense that Raymond Williams was later to describe as a 'whole way of life.'[36] In 1937, recently returned to Cheyne Walk, London, having spent five days in King's Lynn, Kempe's home town, which she had previously only visited on two day-trips, Allen wrote to long-time correspondent and adviser Father Oliger: 'when libraries were closed I walked all day in Lynn, poking into all the corners both of streets and churches. I am a great believer in the living picture as a stimulus to study.'(BMC)

Allen's unpublished papers indicate quite clearly her interest in current events and her ability to make connections between the world around her and the world she studied. An example from unpublished material will serve to illustrate. In the Bryn Mawr collection is a cutting from *The New York Times*, February 14, 1948, with the heading 'The women's vital rôle in the war amid the rubble.' The article by Anne O'Hare McCormick concerns the reconstruction work done in Berlin by women, the changes in women's rôles during and after the war, and the failure to recognise these changes. Her argument was that only the Soviet Union had taken account of the need to rethink issues of gender in relation to changed social circumstances and the absence of men in certain age groups.

Allen takes up this issue of women's rôles and undervalued capacities by beginning a letter, presumably intended for the paper, in which she points out the vitality of earlier German women mystics and the tradition of which they were part. Her objective is to compare 'a modern disastrous situation in Germany' with 'a most remarkable tradition of feminine accomplishment...not paralleled by any other European nation' (BMC) and to remind Germany of its history. Here medieval history is adduced as a source of education for the present.

Allen's inclusivist approach is reflected in her proposal that 'BMK II,' as she refers to the proposed companion to the EETS 212 edition of the Kempe text, be 'the synthesis of Margery the mystic and the woman' (BMC). It is not surprising that *The Book of Margery Kempe* lent itself so much to her imagination, given her belief that the *Book* needed both literary and historical perspective, and an understanding of the connections between the mystical and the social. In 1949 she wrote to Mabel Day of her 'wide ranging desire to make it [BMK II] my magnum opus—in which at least all the absorptions of my various incarnations coalesce, even tho[ugh] not all the methods.'[37]

Five years later she wrote in much the same positive spirit, 'This BMK II curiously sums up all the research I ever did & I feel myself exceedingly fortunate to have it on hand.' Yet the nature and scope of the work were not unalloyed pleasures as is clear in statements such as 'But BMK has buried me alive—almost.' In 1953 a similarly fearful tone is present when she described how far her scope has broadened and that 'even to produce what I supplied for EETS 212 was a nearly killing matter' (BMC).

If there are specific reasons why *The Book of Margery Kempe* should be both the best and worst project that Allen could have taken on in terms of her inherently global methodology, then there were also other circumstances that contributed to the magnitude of the project and militated against Allen's ever completing BMK II. These concerned her aims as a scholar, which might be described as guarding unpublished medieval manuscripts and fostering the development of knowledge and history.

The first of these is nicely rendered in a letter from Allen to Helen Gardner only recently made accessible at the Bodleian library. This group of letters between Allen, her friends, and other scholars was placed in the Bodleian by Joan Wake with the proviso that no access be allowed to them until 1992 on the grounds that at the time of their placement in 1967 most of the writers were still alive. This particular letter to Gardner in 1947 expresses Allen's feeling that it is 'wonderfully stimulating' to know 'that there are watchdogs on the field still collaborating on subjects [such] as the edition of Julian.'[38]

This well captures Allen's keen sense of her rôle as guardian of early English manuscripts and her sense of herself, with some others, as a watchdog patrolling the boundaries of scholarship, maintaining scholarly standards. While this was to some extent a self-appointed position, Allen clearly did have the respect and confidence of many people working in the area of medieval literature in her time. There are many letters asking Allen for her advice on what manuscripts were available for editing and study. Students, teachers, publishers and religious believers wrote for advice on which texts to take up, and the state of progress in medieval study in general. This placed enormous pressure on her as she acknowledged to her friends. In 1949 she wrote to Mabel Day that the 'pressure of unprinted work—about which people tend to write me—is trying.'[39]

If Allen set high standards for others to follow, then it is also apparent that she expected to follow them herself. Her commitment to medieval studies involved her in copious letter writing to other scholars, and this she regarded as part of her responsibilities to the scholarly community. Her effort was not always rewarded. As she wrote to Mabel Day, some of the letter writers on whom she spent considerable time and energy dropped by the wayside without producing what had been promised (BMC).

Because of these demands on her time Allen learnt to make letter writing work for her own study. In a fragment in the collection at Bryn Mawr College she explains her policy of writing long letters and of keeping copies. 'I have adopted the policy of going a little far afield for my correspondent, in order to sum up the subject for myself in a statement of what I now thinks [sic] which I can later use' (BMC). From this policy designed to help others, while clarifying her ideas for her own use, comes the extensive archival material that exists today.

As self-appointed watchdog on medieval matters, Allen often found herself at odds with individual scholars. Hirsh touches on the disagreement between herself and Professor E. J. Arnould, which came to a head around 1947 when the latter, then holding a chair of French at Trinity College, Dublin, turned to Allen for advice on the edition of Rolle's *Melos*, on which he began work in 1937. In the middle of the following year, 1948, Arnould again wrote to Allen complaining that it had come to his attention that a Professor Gabriel M. Liegey was also working on the *Melos*, expecting to publish on it soon. The tone of Arnould's letter is aggrieved and appeals to what he clearly perceives as Allen's high scholarly standards. He expects the other work on Rolle to be inferior and hopes that Allen will somehow intervene or side with him. 'I trust you will understand why I am so anxious to have your advice on this matter' (BMC). The correspondence, however, did not go the way that Arnould had hoped. Allen harboured memories of his earlier research that she had found defective. In accusation and counter accusation the more painful side of moral guardianship is revealed.[40]

Apart from such disagreements, there is no doubt that generally Allen's influence was benign and productive. She consoled herself that though her publication rate slowed down, 'I have at least done a lot of I think helpful collaboration by correspondence.'[41] Such collaboration is attributable to a variety of general factors, including geography, the Second World War, and to Allen's own character. A illuminating fragment of a letter remains in which she directly canvasses her own work methods in relation to the Oneida community and its influences.

> You know of course I am not in the least gregarious, tho devoted to many friends. But to me scholarship has always been something very individual—as religion w[o]uld be (wherein I would not relish the old OC [Oneida Community]).The analogy of the OC shows what can be done by corporate action, and I realise I would gain many advantages by being more gregarious. But then for research I would lose independence…many years now of having all sorts of persons to ask my help—or I ask theirs—or to some degree collaborate (at a distance generally) with others in my field—makes me feel one has to know the other long and well before the full contingencies can come to light—hence I am wary about human judgments now—until the time element has had a good chance to test….[42]

Here is the kernel of some of the difficulties Allen experienced as an independent scholar, working outside an institutional base, yet vitally connected with the world of medieval scholarship. Fiercely protective of her own reputation, to the extent that she refused to allow her name to be mentioned in general acknowledgments if she were unsure of the soundness of the author's particular arguments, Allen prized her own independence yet often could not help getting involved when it might have been wiser to keep a distance. So her judgement, while meticulously cautious, was sometimes flawed.

In this sense although Hirsh has correctly identified Allen as more sinned against than sinning in the difficult production of the EETS volume, part of the problems can be attributed to Allen's fierce sense of intellectual guardianship and her own intellectual diffidence. These factors contributed to the problems of EETS 212, which need to be rehearsed briefly as a corrective to the picture of Allen as victim of the situation. After Allen had identified the manuscript, the next stage in the saga, which Hirsh has described as 'the single greatest misjudgment of her academic career,'[43] and which no doubt contributed to her later caution, was to offer collaboration on the project to Sanford Meech. This offer seems to have been made from a series of motives, one of them being Allen's wish to encourage young and promising scholars, Meech having come to her attention from their collaboration on the *Middle English Dictionary*. Meech had also asked her advice on a manuscript topic. In her rôle as supporter and nurturer of medieval scholars it was consistent that a discovery like the Kempe manuscript be shared.

Yet, at another level, it also seems that Allen lacked confidence in her own ability. In a letter written to Meech in early 1935 Allen mentions two things not widely discussed. First, there is Allen's reference to her lack of confidence in transcribing a medieval manuscript: 'I felt nervous transcribing myself, clear as it looks, because of the twirls at the end of the letters, some of which were to be disregarded I knew.'[44] While there is perhaps an element of modesty here designed to make the less-well-known scholar comfortable, Allen's anxiety is consistent with the fact that throughout her scholarly life she made much use of other scholars to transcribe material for her. J. A. Herbert, from the British Library, is the most obvious example here; Allen was encouraging him to produce transcriptions for her when he was well into his 70s.

The second interest this letter has for the production of the EETS volume is that it reveals a third hand in the enterprise, a revelation that comes as a shock to the modern reader. Allen wrote that she was eager to see Meech 'for a little mutual congratulation on this exciting collaboration in which we are all *three* embarked' (my emphasis); in the same letter comes the explanation, 'I am so glad that Mrs Meech is a collaborator.'[45] If later developments were to see Meech's name as the only one acknowledged as editor, with Allen providing notes and introduction, it seems that completely absent from the picture is the silent woman, Meech's wife. Given that we only discover this from the Allen papers, the question still remains as to exactly what Mrs Meech contributed to the EETS text. More generally, this incident attests to the unsung rôles of the wives of male scholars in the early parts of the twentieth century.

Undoubtedly, Allen felt marginalised, pushed from the position of being joint editor to provider of individual notes. Yet in all the controversy that followed it seems clear that if Allen had taken on the whole project herself, this would not have happened. Trying to play honest broker, A. W. Pollard, Director of EETS, replied to Allen's complaints in November 1935 'It was a great disappointment to me that you were unable to do all that was needed for the publication of Margery's journal yourself' (BMC).

The EETS record was, however, that as Allen had introduced Meech, he was to edit the text, Allen to provide notes and introduction. Again part of the problem seems to have been assumptions regarding the scholarly community, that interests would be shared more than they were, that there would be a level of personal disinterest between scholars. When Allen wrote of EETS's responsibility to her, Pollard reminded her that EETS too had expectations, one of these being that she and Meech would collaborate. As it happened all parties realised that they would have benefited from a formal recording of rôles and responsibilities from the outset. Instead, informal agreements and understandings left everyone uncertain, providing a recipe for acrimony. Given the emergence of academic professionalism, and the development of academic careerism, it was no longer appropriate to produce Middle English texts based on gentlemanly agreement and assumptions.

Another factor complicating the issue was Allen's relationship with the manuscript's owner, Colonel Butler-Bowdon. When the idea of a modernised popular version was mooted, it first appeared that Allen would produce it herself. As the Colonel became more interested in the text, however, Allen wrote to him suggesting that he take on the job. Having done so, and effectively passed on the responsibility, Allen could not help criticising and offering advice to which the Colonel did not take kindly and which he construed as interference.

There seems little doubt that neither Meech nor Butler-Bowdon appreciated Allen's interventions or comments. While Allen's continued interest in the linguistic aspects of the scholarly edition and the modernised version is understandable and completely consistent with her watchdog rôle, it is also possible to sympathise with those who tackled the projects given to them only to find that their interpretations were open to frank criticism and debate from the person who had encouraged them to take up the job in the first place.

It seems evident to me, as it did to Hirsh, that Allen's gender played a part in the difficulties she experienced with Butler-Bowdon and Meech. The combination of personal factors and gender contributed to Allen's situation. One does not need too keen an imagination to see how differently the two gentlemen might have responded to advice from a more experienced *man* who was as highly respected as Allen was.

> Finally, Hope was a woman. Nowhere explicitly referred to, this fact seems to me to have influenced Meech's behavior throughout; it is simply impossible to believe that he would have treated a senior male colleague as he treated her.[46]

If circumstances surrounding the publication of EETS 212 were not the high point of Allen's scholarly career, then *The Book of Margery Kempe* can in other ways be seen as encapsulating both the strengths and the weaknesses, the light and the shade of Allen's scholarly methods. In many ways what Allen described as the multifaceted nature of the *Book* was conducive to Allen's own wide interests. The fact that the text concerns a lay woman, highly devout in her practices, yet controversial, apparently illiterate yet well informed, who contributes information about the town in which she lived, spoke very much to Allen's own interests.

Here was the need for thorough local histories of Norfolk and Lynn, which she was at pains to encourage. The text also needed detailed understanding of religious history and of Continental mysticism and appealed at many levels to both general and local knowledge. Allen also took into account literary and rhetorical dimensions of the *Book*, arguing that it be seen as propaganda, as part of Kempe's aim at sainthood.[47]

When Allen wrote of the second volume of *The Book of Margery Kempe* as her magnum opus, as bringing all her absorptions together, she described how fruitful she found the project. Two images that Allen uses illustrate her sense of the positive and negative aspects of this. On the one hand there is the sheer excitement of discovery, the enthusiasm and intellectual growth that Allen clearly experienced in the twenty-six years she spent researching the manuscript: 'I sent you yesterday a fearful budget—to demonstrate my difficulties in composition through my mind sprouting like a potato brot from the cellar, when anything comes up that interests me.'[48] The image of the potato brought from the darkness of the cellar into the light, alive with new growth, well illustrates the sense of Allen's delight. To read the papers in the Allen archives is to marvel at how many areas Allen found herself researching, how many byways she found herself investigating. Her research is prodigious and inspires awe.

On the other hand sits the indisputable fact that the second volume was never produced, and although she writes of leaving her notes for others to follow, Allen's own knowledge is simply not reproducible. Her self-awareness told her of her weakness here: 'I realise that if I were dealing with money instead of research, I would be a defaulter who didn't balance my books, I am so much behind.' Her image of herself as a financial defaulter is mirrored in other comments in which, for example, she acknowledges 'I am as irresponsible as a child at times in giving way to enthusiasms which only time will dispell' (BMC).

This criticism came from outside as well as from within. It is evident in the remarks of those who knew and admired her. A. C. Baugh wrote to her in 1953 concerning 'BMK II,' 'After all there must be an end to revision sometime' (BMC). A few years earlier, in 1949, Day had written passing on C. T. Onions' inquiry about BMK II in terms likely to touch Allen's conscience:

> what he really wants badly to know clearly [is] when you will be able to get down to Vol. II in bitter earnest. He is afraid the time will never come. So many of our publications are unfinished because the editors never get beyond the text! Some of them have been handed on to a later generation to finish. (BMC)

From a slightly different perspective another friend offered the advice in 1939 that 'I think you bother too much about every single point....I think you are too much out to explain everything.' While one of the concerns here was that Allen attempted to describe the indescribable, to make the metaphysical comprehensible, the remarks are nevertheless consistent with those that feared that Allen was too wide ranging, that she simply took on too much, thus rendering completion impossible. In this sense, Allen was indeed a child of the 'perfectionists,' intellectually and emotionally.

Perhaps one of the first people to point out the problems endemic in Allen's approach was Father Herbert Thurston, who in 1928 reviewed Allen's *Writings Ascribed to Richard Rolle* and pointed out both the long-term unimpeachable value of Allen's work and the drawbacks:

> the ever-growing army of serious girl students who are keen about success in the research work which was formerly the monopoly of their male rivals will not be wanting in appreciation of what Miss Allen has achieved. We are tempted to think that she has perhaps been even too meticulous, too conscientious, in her hunting down of every recorded text and every reference which could afford a clue to the elucidation of the rather obscure problems of Richard Rolle's literary activities. The standard she sets would seem to demand too large a proportion of man's limited working days to be practicable for any but a very few.[49]

Wake's obituary of Allen captures this shared sense of Allen as perfectionist. Asked to say something about Allen 'on the personal side,' Joan Wake wrote the following:

> Hope Allen was small and slight—not much above five feet in height—pale, with fair straight hair and light blue eyes. She dressed quietly, was undemonstrative, entirely unaffected, and might easily have escaped notice in a crowd, but a second glance would surely have arrested attention, for she was a person of great independence and force of character. In the 1930's she was wearing a long black cape and a black beret. "I saw Hope Allen this morning," said one of the dons at Newnham, "flitting about Cambridge like the ghost of Erasmus." (BMC)

In Allen's wide-ranging interests, her ability to follow diverse lines of inquiry, to shoot off in different directions, lie her strength and her weakness. Her contributions were significant, her energy remarkable, her scholarship underestimated. An example to future scholars, Allen provided her own estimate of future work that is still relevant and which in many ways characterises the trends that were to develop around *The Book of Margery Kempe*:

> If I am not able to present my facts so as to bring out their full interest, I have at least collected them, and someone who comes after me is likely to be able to use them for a stimulating study of the sort of literary history which is as much history as it is literature, and as much literature as it is history.[50]

Notes

1. Bodleian, MS. English Letters c.212: 119. Allen explains that the three scholars who were first offered the manuscript were Dom Huddleston, Dr M. R. James, and Allen's cousin Evelyn Underhill. Allen also suggests that she offered the opportunity to a scholar from King's Lynn, Kempe's birthplace, Dorothy Everett, who also declined. The assumption that the other scholars were presumed to hold, that whoever 'wrote' the manuscript must have been an anchoress, arises from the ascription on Henry Pepwell's 1521 edition, 'Here endeth a shorte treatyse of a deuoute ancres called Margery kempe of Lynne,' although it is not clear why this should necessarily have led others to preclude the possibility that Butler-Bowdon's manuscript was Margery Kempe's.

2. John C. Hirsh, *Hope Emily Allen: Medieval Scholarship and Feminism* (Norman, Oklahoma: Pilgrim Books, 1988).

3. Hirsh discusses this stage of her career in more detail, 1988, pp. 51 & 99.

4. Ibid., p.113.

5. Butler-Bowdon's ownership of the manuscript and his own rôle in the first modernisation are stories the detail of which is beyond the scope of this book. Chapter four, however, which looks at the reception of the first versions of the *Book*, does include two intriguingly different accounts of how the manuscript came to be discovered in the Butler-Bowdon household.

6. Hirsh provides the best published account of this, 1988, pp.113–114.

7. The three most substantial collections of this material are in Bryn Mawr College, where Allen completed her undergraduate degree, the Bodleian Library, and the Northamptonshire Record Office (NRO), founded by Allen's close friend, Joan Wake.

8. The significance of Allen's relationship with Ellis and Joan Wake is the subject of the next chapter.

9. The home of the Victoria and Albert Museum in London.

10. Bodleian, MS. ENG. MISC. c. 484.

11. *Time and Tide*, 17 May 1941, as held in the Joan Wake collection in the Northamptonshire Record Office.

12. John C. Hirsh, 1988, p.126.

13. John Humphrey Noyes, *History of American Socialisms* (New York: Dover Publications, 1966), pp. 625–6.

14. Ibid., p. 626.

15. Ibid., p. 639.

16. Bodleian, MS. English Letters c. 212.

17. I am indebted initially to Sue Ellen Holbrook for this connection.

18. The letter from Wake to Allen, dated April 22 1930, takes the form of a question, and the reference reads in full 'Have you read V. Woolf's "A Room of One's Own'?...Too self-conscious and dramatic, but quite excellent in parts, and a great improvement on that silly book Orlando' (NRO). It is amusing to note Wake's disparaging remarks on *Orlando*, and entirely understandable that Wake would take a dim view of a book that parodies Englishness, class and history, given Wake's own proud family history. Wake's older brother, Sir Hereward Wake, was the 13th Baronet, heir to a family that traced its origins back to the

Wacs of the twelfth century. See Peter Gordon's compendious history, *The Wakes of Northamptonshire* (Northamptonshire: Northamptonshire Libraries and Information Service, 1992).

19. Bodleian, MS. Engl. Misc. c. 484.

20. Ibid.

21. Bodelian, MS. English Letters. c. 212.

22. Bodleian, MS. Engl. Misc. c. 484.

23. See also the correspondence between Allen and George Bernard Shaw published at http://libwww.syr.edu/digital/collections/c/Courier/0.2.htm, where Allen tries to protect the reputation of the Oneida community from attention she perceived as sensationalist.

24. Bodleian, MS. Engl. Misc. c.484.

25. Ibid.

26. Charles Nordhoff, *The Communistic Societies of the United States: From Personal Visit and Observation* (New York: Dover Publications Inc, 1966), p. 289.

27. Ibid., p. 290.

28. Ibid., p. 292. I take the comment about him being 'a respector of persons' to suggest that what he said might alter according to whom he spoke, a criticism that implies that one ought to speak the truth regardless of audience.

29. Ibid.

30. Bodleian, ME. Engl. Misc. c. 484. Allen's father was 50, her mother 41, her brother 10 when Allen was born. Partly because of her mother's ill health, Allen's father's sister became her 'second mother.'

31. Hirsh, 1988, p. 9.

32. M. Carey Thomas cited in Helen Lefkowitz Horowitz, *The Power and Passion of M. Carey Thomas* (New York: Alfred A. Knopf, 1994), p. 317.

33. Ibid., p. 321, where Horowitz quotes from M. Carey Thomas, 'Should the Higher Education of Women Differ from That of Men?' *Educational Review*, 21 (1901): 1–10. In the Bodleian Library collection there is also a draft of a rather confused letter from Allen to *The Times* arguing that the models of Harvard and Radcliffe should not be used to support arguments against permitting women to take degrees at Cambridge. While the specificities of her argument are not clear, the intention is: to reject those arguments against women's full participation in higher education, to set the record straight about her own country's attitude towards these issues, and to prevent arguments about American positions being used against women in England.

34. See Lee Patterson, 'On the Margin: Postmoderism, Ironic History, and Medieval Studies,' *Speculum*, 65, 1990, p.105.

35. See William Benzie, *Dr. F. J. Furnivall: Victorian Scholar Adventurer* (Norman, Oklahoma: Pilgrim Books, Inc, 1983), and David Matthews, *The Making of Middle English: 1765–1910* (Minneapolis: University of Minnesota Press, 1999), chapter 6.

36. Raymond Williams, *Culture* (Glasgow: Fontana Paperbacks, 1981), p. 11.

37. Bodleian, MS. English Letters c. 212.

38. Bodleian, MS. English Letters d. 268.

39. Bodleian, MS. English Letters c. 212.

40. The Allen papers at BMC, in the Bodleian and in the Northamptonshire Record Office's Joan Wake collection reveal how some of these disagreements continued after Allen's death.

Edmund Colledge and Allen fell out over the disputed whereabouts of a manuscript. When Allen died and papers were lodged with BMC, Colledge went there, partly expecting to find the manuscript, it seems, and the collection still contains comments by him on the merits of her work. Given Allen's own often less-than-flattering comments about Colledge, his advice about the dispensable nature of some of the papers, and his presence in this capacity in the collection are disturbing.

41. Bodleian, MS. Engl. Misc. c. 484.
42. Ibid.
43. John C. Hirsh, 1988, p. 113.
44. Bodleian, MS. English Letters c. 212.
45. Ibid. Again, like the story of Butler-Bowdon's ownership, the story of Meech's rôle, as seen through information from his perspective, is still untold.
46. John C. Hirsh, 1988, p. 127.
47. Allen wrote to Mabel Day in February 1938, 'my line-by-line study of the work this winter has convinced me that Margery expected to be a saint, and that in all likelihood the book was prepared for prospective hagiography....Considerable annotation has to be added to bring this out.' In another fragment she wrote 'It must never be forgotten that hers was a work of active propaganda, not literature, or, in the ordinary sense, reminiscence' (BMC).
48. Letter to Mabel Day, March 17, 1949. Bodleian, MS. English Letters c.212.
49. Fr. Herbert Thurston, review of *Writings Ascribed to Richard Rolle*, in *Month*, 1928, 369–371.
50. Bodleian, MS. Engl. Misc. c. 484.

Chapter 3

'The Three Daughters of Deorman': Scholarship and Community

Reading about the production of *The Book of Margery Kempe* for the Early English Text Society is a moving experience. John C. Hirsh's description of the anguish and hurt Hope Emily Allen felt is an important contribution to a history of scholarship that includes the emotional as well as the intellectual and acknowledges the domestic and personal aspects that are part of any writing, no matter how objective that scholarship might be. It is distressing to see the excitement and enthusiasm of discovery end up in recrimination, to see Allen's confidence eroded, her energy evaporate. It is disappointing not to see the long-dreamed-of second volume. Some aspects of the story of Allen's involvement in the production of the *Book* are depressingly familiar in feminist history. We read of aspirations thwarted, of struggles in climates and cultures, which, while dedicated to understanding history, to humanism, also made it very difficult for women to succeed and develop. It is all too familiar.

Yet alongside this it is possible to set a picture of Allen that acknowledges that no more than Eileen Power, the Cambridge medieval historian, was she 'alone as a woman in her field.'[1] Another side of her story reveals the enormously positive interactions between Allen and her friends and collaborators, the genuine love and affection that existed among them and the tremendous benefits these communities conferred on the scholarship of those involved. Allen was not alone in her endeavours, not isolated in her work, in spite of the fact that she did not enjoy the benefits that many current writers and critics do as a result of working in tertiary institutions, with other colleagues, teaching and interacting with students. In this chapter I present a happier story of women's scholarship and cultural production, of the inspirational links forged between scholars, and between women as intellectual workers in particular. While feminist analysis has often focussed on the problems and struggles of women writers, there are also stories of collaboration to celebrate that are truly pleasurable. Allen's own understanding of her interactions with others is also important to the history of scholarship and provides a way of challenging the persistence of the myth of the individual author that sustains the misrepresentation of the reality of authorship as a solitary practice.

When Hope Allen announced the discovery of the manuscript of the Kempe text in *The Times* on 27 December, 1934, she directly testified to her sense of scholarly community and her active engagement with it. The letter began, 'It was said regretfully (not long ago) by a distinguished historian that in the Middle Ages old ladies did not write their reminiscences. The reminiscences of a medieval old lady have lately come to light….' The 'distinguished historian' in question was F. M. Powicke, who sent Allen a copy of his chapter 'Loretta, Countess of Leicester,' inscribed 'with the writer's thanks and good wishes.'[2] Powicke's chapter, in which he specifically acknowledges Allen's help and advice, laments the lack of information about women such as Eleanor of Aquitaine and Loretta, daughter of William of Briouze, 'one of the most powerful barons in the Anglo-Norman state.' 'If some of these could have…[dictated their reminiscences], we should know more about the times in which they lived than we can ever hope to learn from chronicles and records,' wrote Powicke. The incident provides a demonstration of Allen's involvement in the scholarly community and the way that her work, though produced independently, was part of a dialogue with others. In collaborating with Powicke, she facilitated his work, which, in turn, provided ways of reviewing her own work.

While Allen was later less certain that the Kempe manuscript, discovered a year after the Powicke article was published, constituted reminiscence, part of Powicke's point concerning the absence of women from history was very much to the forefront of Allen's thinking and a strong element in her research. Another scholar's observation that she noted further serves to illustrate this point. In 1943 Allen quoted a review by Christopher Morley of Trevelyan's *English Social History* published two months earlier, in February. The remark that struck her was one that echoes Powicke's yet is more specific about the rôle of women in history. 'I have often said to myself that the ideal historians would be old women, since they have the seeing eye for the fulcrum details on which the weights of life are swung.'[3]

However quaint this formulation might seem sixty years later in its essentialising and in its kindly meant but inherently patronising attitude towards 'old women,' both Morley and Powicke point out the absence from history of certain kinds of information. Allen's attraction to these observations is understandable. A major part of her research was precisely the discovery of a text dictated by a medieval woman,[4] which Allen sought to make available and comprehensible. In this way she tried to add to what was known about medieval English life, to add the dimension of social life, and women's lives previously neglected. As a female literary historian, working with other scholars, Allen brought a perspective to bear on her work that was concerned with social context and seeing 'the fulcrum details on which the weights of life are swung.' Allen's recording of these two observations testifies to her own accretive and collaborative work process and to her specific and self-conscious interests in women's histories in their social contexts.

For Allen, the sense of community that began with an extended family and the Oneida environment included many different groups of others.[5] Allen was part of a group of independent woman scholars who debated and shared information through lengthy letters. She collaborated with Joan Wake, the founder of the Northamptonshire Record Society, to encourage and stimulate the development of local history in Norwich and Northampton. She was also part of the laborious team effort behind the *Middle English Dictionary*. She was also concerned with local history in a different sense, through her work concerning the indigenous people, the Indians around Oneida. She attempted to record the oral history of the fragmenting groups, demonstrating an awareness of their situation in Anglo-America. On Independence Day in 1945 Allen's thoughts were not only with the commemoration of white settlement and independence from the British empire but with those whose existence in America predated the seventeenth century. She wrote to Mabel Day[6] that 'Today I celebrated the 4th by picking up a beautiful Indian arrowhead in the 'Sales Office' garden—like a V sign,'[7] combining an awareness of Indian history with American independence and the waning of the war in Europe. Intersections such as this one and interconnections were a feature of the way Allen worked. A refusal to compartmentalise or to adhere to boundaries contributed to Allen's problems with Sanford Brown Meech and Colonel Butler-Bowdon over EETS 212 and the modernised version but was also part of the foundation of Kempe studies. Allen's particular interests mark a shift in understandings of the kinds of issues that might be a proper part of textual analysis.

While Allen was an independent scholar for most of her life, an amateur rather than a professional in the sense that she chose where and what she would work on, she did not work alone. Thanks to Allen's relatives and to her executor Nita Scudder Baugh and to Joan Wake, there is a substantial amount of archival matter that illustrates just how closely Allen was connected to a number of men and women working in England and Europe when she herself was in America. Community was clearly important to Allen who, like other women of the time, worked outside university hierarchies, following their own intellectual pursuits for the benefit of themselves and others. For all of these women working outside the reward system that operates through salary and status, the pursuit of knowledge for its own sake, independence, and self-esteem provided different kinds of rewards.

While most of the long-term friends with whom Allen corresponded were women working on similar areas to her own, there are many examples of letters between Allen and male scholars on medieval topics. One particular set of correspondence illustrates an interesting friendship Allen developed through letters with Pater Livier Oliger, a Franciscan priest in Rome. His letters indicate how a contemporary saw her and how scholarship thrived and survived long distances through letter writing. Originally Allen and Oliger shared a mutual interest in medieval Catholicism, and their relationship developed into one that by the time of Oliger's death was closer than might have been expected of a 'christian agnostic,' as Allen saw herself (BMC), and a Franciscan teacher and scholar. On December 12, 1931, Oliger wrote a reference for Allen, referring to having known her for eight or nine years. In doing so he made both scholarly and personal comments on her application. 'Miss Allen has always made the most favorable impression on me, both as a character and as a scholar: in her morals and habits serious and painstaking in her literary enterprises, endowed with an unusually strong will in pursuing a scientifical question.'[8]

By 1950 this personal dimension was evidently developing in their correspondence: 'I was very interested in what you have to say about your personal position and disposition,' wrote Oliger, 'and you reveal what I always guessed, namely that you prefer a good book to cosmetics and fashionable dress' (BMC). In a 1946 letter to Day in the Bodleian library, Allen confirms this image of herself, declaring 'I dress since 1932 almost entirely in pass me downs from an intimate friend—and I feel free to spend the saving on books.'[9]

Later that year Oliger sent Allen a photograph of himself at the golden jubilee celebration of his priesthood, and in November 1950 Oliger wrote about their illnesses and their different religious beliefs. These newly released letters[10] shed more light on a mystery identified by Hirsh. According to family tradition, Allen was reported to have received letters from a long-time clerical friend on his deathbed, asking her of her religious beliefs. According to Hirsh, 'Hope had none that would comfort him but was reluctant to write under such circumstances. Distressed by the question but unwilling, indeed unable, to lie, she delayed answering until he died.' Hirsh correctly surmised that this clerical friend was Oliger as the latest bundle of letters reveals. Not having seen these letters when he wrote his biography, Hirsh interpreted the family anecdote as setting 'a certain mark on the relationship, correct and friendly, courteous and controlled, but not close in any personal sense.'[11] The incident seen in context of the new information is capable of a slightly different inflection. The first letter in the new collection was written when Oliger was ill but still capable of writing. He demonstrates a clear anxiety for Allen and implies that he is aware of her agnosticism or at least the fact that she did not share his faith. More importantly, his letter suggests that this was, and had been, a matter of concern to him. His letter is part admonition, part plea.

> Turn to God your thoughts and your heart. Pray to Him that he might bestow on you His Light and His Grace for the benefit of your soul. I have been praying for many years in this intention and I trust that God will grant what I asked. Excuse me for these lines, which please take as a sign of true friendship.[12]

That Allen might not respond in kind is implied in Oliger's request that she excuse him for the admonition. The intention behind the request is explicit, that it is to be taken 'as a sign of true friendship.'

Oliger's commitment to Allen, at this stage in his life, gives an insight into the impact Allen could have. A few weeks later, on January 7, 1951, Father William O'Connell wrote on behalf of Oliger who by then was very ill and anxious for Allen to pray for him. Three weeks later, on February 1, O'Connell wrote again, this time with news of Oliger's death: 'He kept a wonderful grasp of his mind right until the end; he was still speaking four languages quite fluently and keeping them distinct until the day of his death.'[13] How Allen responded to this is not evident from any available sources, but these letters contain clear testament to her impact on a devout, scholarly man from a background and faith very different to Allen's own.

It may well be, in the absence of any letter from Allen to Oliger in response either to his or O'Connell's letter and with no reference in O'Connell's letter to having heard from Allen that the family story is accurate. Perhaps Allen could not reply in any terms that would comfort the dying man and would not answer in bad faith to her own beliefs. Hirsh's hypothesis is consistent with other evidence about her character. The story and the new material do, however, suggest that the relationship between Allen and Oliger was strong. Connections made through scholarship became friendships. These letters suggest Oliger's heartfelt concern for Allen, sufficient for him, in the last two months of his life, suffering from liver cancer, to have written once himself, to have commissioned someone else to write when he could not and then request her to be informed of his death. There may be elements here of some kind of pastoral rôle being played out by Oliger. The concern may reflect his sense of religious duty towards someone he respected whom he felt to be in spiritual danger. Nonetheless this new information contributes to a picture of the relationship having been more personal or perceived to be more personal, at least from one of the participants' perspective, than has previously been suggested.

While strong relationships were built up between Allen and fellow scholars, none were stronger than between Allen, Joan Wake and Dorothy Ellis.[14] While Allen's work was significant and extensive, it is also clear from her correspondence that she was not alone, either in the sense of working in isolation or in the sense of being unique. Allen, Wake and Ellis had a long and warm friendship, begun from common interests in history and the medieval period. Collecting Allen's papers, initially to send to the Bodleian Library, Wake wrote that one group was particularly significant because 'this batch seems to throw quite a lot of light, not only on Miss Allen's work during those years [1930s], but on the way in which she made personal friends of the scholars she worked with.' In the same letter, now in the Joan Wake collection at Northamptonshire Record Office, she estimates that Allen and Ellis become friends in about 1932, although another letter in the same collection, from Allen to Ellis in 1934 suggests that the two might have known each other longer than that: 'Your coming back to research is like a romance to me—ever since 1913 [1931?] I have been angling for you.'[15]

At any rate, in November 1932 Allen wrote to 'Miss Ellis' that: 'I go to London (115 Cheyne Walk) Sat a.m. Miss Wake has been ill, and it is even possible she may not go to the reception, but I hope she can. I want you to meet her,'[16] and this seems to have been the beginning of a three-way friendship that lasted until Allen's death in 1960, after which Ellis and Wake still communicated. It is entirely characteristic of these three women that they should talk of themselves as 'the three daughters of Deorman,' a label arising from their passion for medieval scholarship. The three daughters of Deorman refers to Allen's theory that the thirteenth-century spiritual guide *Ancren Riwle* was written for three specific women who could be identified as the daughters of Derman or Deorman of London, 'an important Anglo-Saxon thane,' who also had a son called Ordgar. As Hirsh has argued, one of the significant things about Allen's work on *Ancren Riwle* was her emphasis on and interest in the audience rather then the author. He makes the point that 'she achieved a real breakthrough by first asking not "Who wrote the *Ancrene Riwle*" (though that would come in time) but "For whom was it written?'"[17] Allen's research here is consistent with her abiding interests in communities and with the histories of people as well as of ideas.

The label by which the three friends spoke of themselves resonates with images of community, of a self-awareness of the work they were doing, and of the pleasure in their collaboration. The first community of women, the audience of the *Ancren Riwle*, is mirrored in the three scholars who bring them to light. It is entirely typical that Allen's identification of the audience was built on collaboration between herself and Ellis. In the 1935 *PMLA* article, bearing the title 'The 3 Daughters of Deorman,' Allen acknowledges 'Miss D. M. B. Ellis,' who traced Ordgar's heirs through the *Calendar of Charter Rolls* and passed the information on to Allen.

After the publication of *The Book of Margery Kempe*, Wake wrote to Allen about the EETS edition and a review of it in *The Times Literary Supplement*.

> Needless to say I am immensely proud of being associated with it and of your generous acknowledgment of my 'umble suggestion which I see, together with a ref to Dorothy Ellis—on the front page of T. L. S. So there the 3 daughters of Deormund all appear together as they sat on that sofa at 96 Cheyne Walk and as I hope they will be in the flesh together again ere long. (NRO)

Wake's suggestion had been that Kempe's son, referred to in the *Book*, could have been one of the scribes,[18] and the references to Wake and Ellis indicate how much these women worked together and fed off each other's work. That it is the work and the community that is important in this image is evident from the fact that none of them could remember which of them was which daughter of Deorman. Allen wrote to Ellis, 'Are you Emma Christine or Gunhilda? Joan must decide,'[19] and in May 1941 Ellis wrote to Wake thanking her for forwarding Allen's letters 'was I Gunnhilda? or were you?' (NRO) On Ellis' birthday, 3 September of the same year, Ellis and Wake were together writing 'Dear Daughter of Deormund, Greetings from the other two,' with Wake finishing the letter, 'Here this D of D seems to have come to an abrupt conclusion sans finishing with signature—but truth to tell, we have forgotten our right names.'[20] This letter, moving backwards and forwards between Ellis and Wake, encompasses medieval philology, gardening, mutual friends and their illnesses, *The Book of Margery Kempe*, accommodation, and finances. These passages celebrate female friendships, work, and leisure.

The support the two English women gave their American friend is everywhere apparent in their letters as are the connections between the women and their work. In the joint letter, Ellis wrote 'A thousand thanks for Margery—I had bought three more of her....She—that means you—is (which should be "are") even more wonderful and thrilling than I expected,' and in a separate letter Wake, referring to the physical appearance of the EETS edition, wrote of the 'great arrival at the Green Farm!!!![21] Margery has come!!!!!!!! Complete in her brown habit with gold facings' (NRO). Allen wrote to Ellis and Wake of her struggles with the edition, receiving encouragement and support in reply. Each of the women wrote admiringly of the others. After Ellis' visit Wake wrote to Allen 'What a highly intelligent person D. E. is—a very good brain' and went on to lament the fact that her war work was taking her away from scholarship.[22]

The women wrote to each other on the anniversaries of occasions spent together. In January 1941 Wake wrote,

Sitting in the sitting-room window here looking out over the bay below—a rough sea rolling and roaring against the rocks—a bright sun and the sea most gloriously blue and green and the bay laced with white foam—I simply can't resist...taking up my pencil to write to you from this beloved spot of such happy memories on the back of an unpaid bill...

and remembered again in 1944

My dearest Hope, it is Midsummer Day and I must not shall not let it pass without writing to you. What a cause for thankfulness it is that nothing can take our happy memories away from us—and you and I have so many joint ones—that happy time in Cornwall not by any means the least among them for both of us, I think.[23]

While the friends did not see each other very often, the intervening World War II keeping Allen in America, the warmth of their friendship is evident. After seeing her in 1951, Ellis wrote to Allen the following year:

this I can say truly of you and I think of no one else in this world or out of it—not even my mother or Skagie—I do not think a day passes without my thinking of you, remembering you, quoting you (very occasionally, I am afraid), praying for you, or saying to some one "The greatest friend I have is an American woman." (NRO)

While Allen acknowledged the help of Wake and Ellis, Wake also included Allen in her own writing. Most of Wake's work focussed on local history, and in 1944 she wrote to Allen about a book she had just completed. 'Did you find yourself in my *Life of Mr. Longden*? I put you in alright, but *sans* your name' (NRO). Wake had produced *Northamptonshire and Rutland Clergy from 1500* by the Reverend Henry Isham Longden, which included an Introduction ('being a Life of the Author') (1943). In the Introduction it appears that one passage about Longden could have been what Wake referred to. Longden had just received information from one of his friends and correspondents that helped him piece together more information.

> "it is wonderful how all such bits fit in like mosaic work when one begins to put them together." And this it may be supposed, was very much what it meant to him. A name or date or some other fragment of information recovered from an old will or parish register, then another, and another, until a shadowy outline began to emerge, and finally, so far as it could be completed, the picture was complete. To most people, even to most students, this patient collection of a vast number of minute particulars—little as a rule but names and dates—would have been an intolerable drudgery. From him it exercised an eternal fascination, and the result of his labours of nearly sixty years is an organised mass of material of immense value to the student—the dry bones, perhaps, but the essential skeleton of the history of rural society.[24]

If this is a portrait of Allen, then interestingly enough it also sounds like a self-portrait of Wake although Wake modestly denied any claim that she was a historian herself, writing to Allen in 1942, '*Don't* call me a "historian"—I am a cross between a missionary and a ferret that's all.' (NRO)

While the friendships lasted most of their adult lives, they were not always smooth running. Allen and Wake were disappointed that Ellis changed her priorities during and after the war. Ellis wrote to Allen 'I have become a most excellent vegetable-maid, darner, and maker of jams and chutneys! You wouldn't know me.' Referring back to the three of them working together she continued, "'The Three Daughters of Deorman' I am afraid I have sold my birthright—but don't let it be too long before we meet again: the years go so fast' (NRO).

The greatest tension existed between Allen and Wake, and their forty-year friendship was not without its hiccups. Most often Wake objected strongly to Allen giving her advice, particularly about what Britain should do during the war before America had joined the Allies but also about what she should do in her garden and how to look after her health. Sometimes Wake's responses were tolerant and witty.

> Split my infinitives! but I was glad to get 2 good letters from you this a. m....Hang my participles! but I am most pleased you liked your b[irth]d[ay] present—and am most grateful for your criticisms. But I don't grasp your meaning. Send me just 2 examples from my book of bad construction and how it should be done. You once gave me a long and most useful lecture on style. (NRO)

Allen's tendency to 'lecture' Wake was what most annoyed her, perhaps partly because Wake had not had a Bryn Mawr education like Allen nor a Newnham College education like Ellis. At any rate sometimes Wake could not restrain herself from expressing her feelings. Reacting against Allen's forthrightness, Wake wrote that 'I very much resent you instructing me as to my behaviour at this time on what I should or should not grow in my garden,' and at another time 'Your attitude is darned superior you know.' On one particular occasion Wake reacted to advice Allen kept giving her about medication Allen sent to England. The letter's emphases resonate with the sounds of Wake's frustration.

> You treat me as though I were half-witted—and have written me *at least* 8 letters on the subject. I really am *capable* of understanding a plain statement. So please dear Hope *don't do it again.* (NRO)

Generally, however, the friends exchanged ideas freely and frankly. It was perhaps inevitable that strong-minded and intelligent women like these would not always agree with each other and would not pretend that they did. From as early as 1927 their commitment to the relationship is evident. Even at that stage they acknowledged their differences, but Wake wanted to concentrate on their connections: 'Best love, Hope dear, I will think of the things we agree on which are many and fundamental.' In 1939 Wake acknowledged that they were both alike in speaking their minds and that at long distance this led to hurt and disappointment.

> Look here—don't let us spoil things by blurting out everything in our minds when likely to annoy the other. I think we are *both* inclined possibly too much to do this—and the greatest intimacy goes better with some restraints I am sure—even though one may call them conventional. (NRO)

The strength of this community of women scholars is apparent in the letters that span a forty-year period, from the early 1920s to 1960 when Allen died, and correspondence continued between Wake and Ellis. While each worked independently of formal institutions and hierarchies, they all benefited from their collaboration with each other and a vast network of academics and scholars with whom they were in touch. From J. R. R. Tolkien to F. N. Robinson to Eileen Power and Helen Cam, their contacts were spread far and wide, all geared to the ends of gathering data and re-writing history. Their histories were not of wars, although they wrote during two world wars, but the social history of everyday life, which Wake, in particular, was instrumental in establishing through rescuing documents, primary source material, from potential destruction.

If Wake, Allen, and Ellis generally worked outside the university system, then there is no doubt that when academic honours were given them, they took great pleasure from the recognition. Allen was awarded an honorary doctorate in humane letters in 1946 by Smith College, and in 1953 Oxford University awarded Wake an honorary Master of Arts.[25] For both women this recognition was an 'apotheosis,' and when Wake wrote to Allen to describe the event she knew that she wrote to someone who would understand.

> Oh! my dear—having been and felt *such* an outsider all my life—to be inside the fold! it is wonderful—…I have tried to do the work for its own sake, but felt that if there was to be any recognition there was only one kind which I would appreciate as really worth having— i.e., from the academic world, and now it has come and in such a perfect way and I do feel so grateful. (NRO)

Characteristically, this great pleasure did not stop her describing the occasion so as to play down her own importance and to make Allen laugh. The central image is an ironic revision of a ritual traditionally central to a woman's life. 'The whole thing,' she wrote, 'was so absurdly like a wedding without the music, cake and bridegroom,' and then later with a historian's eye on the ceremony she wrote of the undergraduates 'kneeling in rows before the Vice-Chancellor, and being banged on the head with a Bible, while he said "In nomine" (bang) "Dei Patries" (bang), "et Filii" (bang) "et Spiritus Sancti" (bang)—that must go back to the thirteenth century surely.'(NRO)

The lives of these women provide an alternative history to that of men and women working within universities. Outside the institution but connected to it through their writing and their contributions to the work of other scholars, they experienced advantages and disadvantages. While none of them were well off financially, all survived without a full-time salary. Wake had various shares, including some Allen advised her to buy, in the Oneida Corporation, for which she often expressed her gratitude as they consistently made more money than her other shares. There were problems, which the extensive correspondence helped to ameliorate. The tendency to keep on working without imposing or having deadlines imposed was also clearly a disadvantage, for Allen, in particular, who seems not to have published anything after 1942. Against these serious disadvantages must have been the exhilaration of following their own paths, chasing the scholarly hares wherever they went, of working alone but knowing that across the world there were others doing the same: a network of scholars united in their desire to 'Follow Truth and if it leads you to the Gates of Hell, *Knock*' (NRO).

Not only do the letters preserved in the Bryn Mawr Archives, the Bodleian Library, and the Northamptonshire Record Office provide information about this group of independent women scholars, but they also provide information about the conditions under which they worked and in which texts like *The Book of Margery Kempe* were produced. In many of these letters we see the importance of women to each other. Dorothy Ellis and her companion/housekeeper Skay

Mackaig clearly provided Allen with comfort and support in the late 1930s when Allen was struggling with EETS 212 and collaboration with Meech, as she wrote to them in a letter of 1941, addressed to 'My dear Dorothy and Skay.'

> Margery gives me hope. "Daughter you shall sit on your well-stool and think of your woe-stool." That has come back to me over and over, these years of strain. You know better than almost anyone what it has all been because you harboured me during some of the worst moments.(BMC)

Allen continued 'You have now such a situation as staggers the imagination even on medieval lines,' and letters between Allen, Ellis, and Day also provide fascinating pictures of these women's lives during the war. Letter after letter written by Allen between 1940 and 1950 and received by her during this period mention the food and clothing packages that Allen sent to friends in England, sometimes long after it was really necessary. Mabel Day and C. T. Onions were two of the most favoured recipients. On letter-head of the medieval journal *Medium Aevum*, Onions wrote on April 2, 1945, thanking Allen for the 'parcel of goodies' he had received (BMC). As late as 1953 Onions was still receiving dispensations from his ration-free American friend. On an air letter commemorating the coronation of Queen Elizabeth II in 1952, Onions wrote to thank Allen for the present of sugar she had sent him to make jam. Mabel Day too wrote often, thanking Allen for clothes and sugar, remarking in 1948 that her five pounds of sugar had produced two pounds of jam.

If letters between Ellis and Allen are warmest in tone, destabilising the cool, detached scholarly sense of Allen it is easy otherwise to develop, letters between Allen and Day are most informative about social and political events. From Mabel Day come insights into the business of trying to work during the bombing of London. The physical production of EETS 212 takes on a new dimension when Day reports that 'The proofs will have the romantic interest of having been often read to the sound of gun-fire—they have even gone down to the air-raid shelter when the search lights were too inconveniently intersecting overhead' (BMC). In 1939 Day also wrote to Allen with the 'news' that she now has to open her case as she enters 'the B.M. for fear there should be an Irish bomb in it!' (BMC)

From Day, too, came information concerning day-to-day life during the war. In 1940 she returned to London to find a study window 'broken by an adjacent bomb two nights ago' (BMC). While the country might be safer, she wrote, it was not without danger. 'The autumn tints are lovely now in the Chilterns. But when one goes walking in the fields, it is best to step into a wood or under a hedge when planes are passing over, for they *may* come down and machine-gun you. It seems incredible that the world has come to this' (BMC).

After the war Day continued to provide valuable evidence concerning life in England. Still receiving parcels from Allen in 1954, Day had kept a white blouse and given other clothes away. Suffering from arthritis, Day had been put on a strict diet so could only admire, rather than consume, the tinned food. Having thus responded to the presents sent, Day then went on to describe economic factors in a passage worth quoting at length for the vivid picture it suggests of post-war England.

> We who live in flats are having an exciting time now the Government's bill for letting landlords raise their rents has gone through. A Tenants' Assocn took a room at the Maida Vale High School just opposite me and called a meeting of members. They expected about 300 members, and they got over 2000. People had come from all over London and as far as Brighton and Bedford, and after the school was full they blocked the whole roadway (a broad one), and the weight of the crowd was beginning to force the doors when the police arrived and took control. I wonder what will happen. I certainly don't want to pay any more rent for the privilege of having a porter 2 hours a day instead of full time, my landlord having already made a tidy profit by letting the former porter's flat *furnished* for a nice large sum. (BMC)

In 1951 Allen wrote to a mutual friend that she had heard from Mabel Day who had 'just retired from being secretary of EETS (aged 75 but still breaking the ice at Kenwood, to swim at xmas).'[26] The fortitude and energy of these women shine through in their letters to and about each other.

Allen's own letters to her friends reveal other aspects of her character that add to an understanding of her and suggest other facets of this woman who in many ways is characterisable as a blue-stocking. Her awareness of and concern with world politics are evident throughout her letters. She was often anxious about the rôle of America during the war and after it, sometimes apologising for what she felt was a lack of involvement on the part of her country. She expressed guilt for the shortages her English friends experienced in comparison with her own relative comfort. Sending parcels served a variety of purposes for her; it helped her friends in a concrete way but also assuaged some of the guilt she felt at her lack of scholarly output. She felt responsible not only to her friends labouring under difficult circumstances overseas but also to those funding agencies, such as the American Council of Learned Societies, that provided her with financial support through grants. In 1949 she wrote to Onions explaining some of these issues, giving insight into her motivations and her sense of commitment to those with whom she worked and who supported her in diverse ways.

To send parcels in my small way has been a wonderful comfort to me when I have felt so ineffectual much of the last years—browsing and not composing, because I was not yet over the severe strain of the early years of having the responsibility for the BMK—on top of five years earning my living and going abroad on other people's money—i.e. "grants."[27]

Her grasp of the minutiae of other people's daily lives, even when she had not seen them for many years, is striking. Eccentric, fastidious, and impetuous in following the hares of her scholarly imagination Allen may have been, but her correspondence illustrates an intensely practical and worldly woman, considerate of the needs of others. Letters primarily concerned with discussion of medieval manuscripts and etymological debates of fine detail also include homely information. One card to Day in 1947 was turned on its side and the following information typed on the edge, acknowledging the co-existence of the scholarly and the domestic. 'At long last soap flakes came back and I could not refrain from sending you a box—plus bags for your sandwich lunch…I forget if I sent Fels Naptha soap—good for lukewarm water laundry.'[28] The pedantic scholar reveals herself to be a fastidious and thoughtful housekeeper.

Amongst all the letters in England and America are also a number of photographs and sketches. Three will serve to illustrate some of the characteristics of these communities of independent women scholars in the early and middle parts of the twentieth century. The first was presumably sent by Allen to Wake (Fig. 1). It is similar to the formal studio portrait appended by Hirsh to his biography of Allen. Here Allen is every inch the serious young woman scholar, diffident and demure, gentle and lady-like, perhaps most people's idea of an early twentieth-century blue-stocking. The second photograph (Fig. 2) of Joan Wake indicates how different Wake and Allen were in style and size but depicts Wake as she spent many of her days, studying and identifying manuscripts.

The third image (Fig. 3) is a sketch by Joan Wake of herself and Allen, wittily self-mocking by exaggerating the physical differences between them, at her own expense. Attached to the sketch is a letter of 1935 in which Wake writes of just having seen Allen in Oxford where Wake lived. Discussion of a misplaced hot water bottle leads Wake to hope that 'Miss Ellis,' whom Allen is next to see, might have another one. Together again in this letter, the three daughters of Deorman meet, go about their work, and come together again. The sketch refers to Allen's characteristically tactless expression that if 'the worst came to the worst,' presumably meaning if she could not stay anywhere else, then she would return to Wake. Wake, again with characteristic good humour in her dealings with Allen, mocks both herself and Allen, visually representing a literal interpretation of the commonplace expression.

Fig. 1. Hope Emily Allen (NRO)

Fig. 2. Joan Wake with manuscript (NRO)

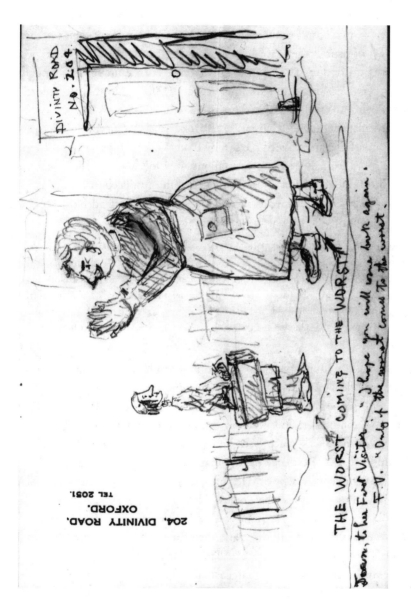

Fig.3. Sketch of Hope Allen and Joan Wake by Wake (NRO)

Set alongside this is a word picture drawn by Joan Wake. At the end of the most substantial of the three books of material on Allen in the Bodleian archives are a series of black and white photographs, including interiors and exteriors of 116 Cheyne Walk, London. Cheyne Walk was at one time co-owned by Allen and Marietta Pallis, a botanist and writer.[29] Initially, Allen owned half of the building that consisted of two coster-monger's cottages knocked together. Later on, under some financial pressure, Allen sold half her half-share in return for use of rooms when she visited London. The photographs themselves are interesting enough, a thoughtfully provided insight into another aspect of Allen's life, a visual record of the kind of environment she inhabited for some time.

One particular photograph shows the back yard of Cheyne Walk, on its reverse a wonderful, allusive word picture by Joan Wake, conjuring up a different Allen to the more formal portrait presentations. In 1966 Wake recalled a summer evening in the yard, about forty years earlier, and the recollection resonates with intimations of Allen and her friends and the power of those friendships. Scribbled in pencil on the photograph's reverse is the following account:

> Backyard of 116 Cheyne Walk looking towards the cottages where coster-mongers lived until M. Pallis bought them and turned them into a studio. In this yard, when Hope had finished her big R. Rolle and I a book of mine, we had a great bonfire of proofs, and danced and sang around it. Marietta, Hope, Mrs Clarke who jumped through the flames, the Cook (Mrs Mott) and Ernie the taxi-driver her friend, and one or two others, coster-mongers—a great party late into a summer night. The wind got up and the burning papers started to fly about—rather alarming.[30]

Such a vivid account provides a good example of the significance of community in Allen's life, while at the same time proving the points of male historians and writers like Powicke and Morley. A concern with context, relationships, communities, and everyday events has traditionally been associated with women, no doubt as much because of social pressures as any inherent or biological imperatives. These are qualities that Wake adds to our understanding of the early-twentieth-century scholar. Her picture is human, alive, trivial yet telling. It is precisely these features that make Allen, Wake, Day, Ellis and others important objects of study. By learning about them, by reading what they wrote to each other, we gain insights into them and their times that are not recorded in the official annals of history. The image of Allen and her friends singing and dancing around the fire, celebrating their intellectual productivity, is an image to set alongside the formal presentation. These 'reminiscences' provide us with the kind of information to which Allen dedicated part of her life, and the absence of which Powicke and Morley lament. Here is the drama in life and scholarship that needs to be recognised. Here is the intellectual and social climate that saw the identification and early promulgation of *The Book of Margery Kempe*.

Notes

1. Maxine Berg, *A Woman in History: Eileen Power, 1889–1940* (Cambridge: Cambridge University Press, 1996).
2. F. M. Powicke, 'Loretta, Countess of Leicester,' *Historical Essays in Honour of James Tait* (Manchester: Manchester University Press, 1933). There is a signed copy of this paper in the Allen archives at Bryn Mawr College.
3. Bryn Mawr College Special Collections, hereafter (BMC).
4. As Sue Ellen Holbrook pointed out on an earlier draft of this, it is interesting that Allen should see Kempe as an old woman, given that this is not the sense of Kempe that arises from her book.
5. The previous chapter contains an account of Allen's family background including her family's involvement with the Oneida Community, one of the experiments in stirpiculture or eugenics, combining religious and communistic values, that is now part of the history of American communitarian societies of the eighteenth and nineteenth centuries.
6. Secretary to the Early English Text Society.
7. Bodleian, MS. English Letters c. 212.
8. Bodleian. MS. English Letters d. 268.
9. Bodleian, MS. English Letters c. 212.
10. Bodleian, MS. English Letters d. 268. There were letters collected by Joan Wake after Allen's death, deposited in the Bodleian, not put on public access until 1995.
11. John C. Hirsh, 1988, p. 68.
12. Bodleian, MS. English Letters d. 268.
13. Ibid.
14. Miss D. M. B. Ellis was one of Newnham College, Cambridge's, first female graduates, an independent scholar, interested in local histories, and a conservative reformist.
15. Hirsh dates the relationship from the early 1930s (1988, p. 86), but Allen was at Newnham in 1910 so might have met Ellis around that time.
16. Northamptonshire Record Office, hereafter (NRO).
17. Hirsh, 1988, p. 45.
18. Butler-Bowdon disputed this and could not really see the importance of it, and Meech debates the notion in his introduction (1940, vii–viii).
19. Bodleian, MS. Engl. Misc. d. 484.
20. Ibid.
21. The Green Farm, Cosgrove, Buckinghamshire, which Wake rented from 1937.
22. Ibid. Apart from making jams and chutney and doing her own sewing and darning as part of the necessity of making ends meet, it is not clear what Ellis was doing at a more general level in this 'war work' except that it left little or no time for scholarship.

23. Joan Wake's mother was Catherine St Aubyn of St. Michael's Mount in Cornwall. Wake often went to visit her mother's family at the Mount or at Nanjizal, Porthcurnow. Allen visited in 1937 and worked on *The Book of Margery Kempe* there.

24. *Northamptonshire and Rutland Clergy from 1500*, by Rev. Henry Isham Longden, with an Introduction (being a Life of the Author) by Joan Wake, Vol. XV (Northampton: Archer and Goodman, 1943), p. xxviii.

25. Leicester University awarded her an honorary doctorate in 1959.

26. Bodleian, MS. English Letters d. 268.

27. Bodleian, MS. English Letters c. 212.

28. Bodleian, MS. English Letters c. 218.

29. Marietta Pallis painted Allen's portrait and was another long-term friend of Allen's and Wake's, although the Northamptonshire Record Office contains letters in which Wake complains bitterly about what she felt to be Pallis' unreasonableness. Again, strong-minded and talented women sometimes clashed.

30. Bodleian, MS. Engl. Misc. c. 484. John C. Hirsh (1988, p. 98) also quotes this passage for different purposes.

Chapter 4

'A Literary Event': Reporting *The Book of Margery Kempe*, 1934–1943

Two important medieval manuscripts were actually identified in 1934. That year brought us, as well as the Kempe manuscript, the manuscript now known as the Winchester Malory after Winchester College Library, where it was found. In relation to that discovery we have the charming account of W. F. Oakeshott of how he came to be the one to recognise the manuscript for what it was. His area of particular interest at the time was the bindings of the college's books and manuscripts, and this is where the story begins.

> The safe where the manuscripts were kept was not in the gallery but in the Warden's bedroom. This was indeed the *penetralia* of the Warden's lodgings, and it had already a legendary reputation with me, since not so many years before a knowledgeable visitor who had made his way into it had recognized, in the bedside mat, a magnificent piece of Tudor tapestry.[1]

Only some weeks later does Oakeshott realise that the Arthurian material contained in the safe is Malory's and announce the identification in *The Telegraph*. Following this report, Eugene Vinaver, already working on an edition of Malory's work, arrived at the college but was initially prohibited from doing more than look at the manuscript, until Oakeshott, by then regretting his hasty announcement, could contact the Warden of the college, Sir Frederic Kenyon. Oakeshott's account of what happened next is relevant in terms of its similarities and differences from the identification of the Kempe manuscript.

> Kenyon pressed me strongly to produce an edition of the text. He had an intense belief in what he called "discoverer's rights." But I soon decided that this made very little sense, seeing that Vinaver had already the background which I should have to begin to acquire. I skimmed the cream quite unscrupulously in an article for *The Times*.[2]

Once again, the discoverer of the manuscript does not go on to be the editor of the text although for quite different reasons and in quite different circumstances.

Seen from a twenty-first-century academic perspective, Oakeshott's modesty and his minimal sense of self-interest are refreshing given our own 'publish or perish' values. In addition, his account hints at the rôle played by the public press. It is from *The Telegraph* that the world, including Malory scholars, hears about the discovery, and it is *The Times* that develops the information. Thanks to Hope Allen, we have even more information as to how the press played a key part in the reception and dissemination of the other 1934 manuscript, the Kempe text, to a wide general audience.

In the midst of the confusions, the intricacies, the duplications, and the false starts that are the seven boxes of Allen's notes in the Bryn Mawr College Archives, sit two scrapbooks of newspaper cuttings from a clippings agency, collated by the ever-conscientious Allen.[3] The newspaper headlines of the 1930s and 1940s position the Kempe text in different contexts.[4] Into the unpublished private projections for future work intrude these markers from the public world of newspapers. Here are windows onto the discovery; here are stories recounting its importance then, stories that are contradictory, illuminating, and misinformative.

'The old book on the shelf' comes alive as perceived by reviewers and critics of the time responding to the publication of the modernised version edited by Colonel Butler-Bowdon. In these scrapbooks is the beginning of a history of reception, a case study of the critical reception of a text, popular and specialised. Bounded at one end by the moment of the text's discovery, bounded at the other by the researcher's own time, *The Book of Margery Kempe* offers a case study of criticism in the twentieth and twenty-first centuries. From the pre-war period of the mid-1930s to today, the reception and criticism of the *Book* intersect with major cultural and aesthetic concerns of those decades. The newspaper cuttings illustrate that the discovery of the manuscript was greeted as significant from the beginning and hailed as a literary event.

Yet what exactly did the papers say? How was the *Book* initially understood and received? The 'life tale of 1437 feminist'? Autobiography? Biography? 'Picture of England 500 years ago'? 'A library discovery,' 'a literary event,' an 'outstanding volume,' 'among the English classics'? Papers religious (*Light*, the *Catholic Herald*) and secular (the *Evening Standard*, *The New York Times Book Review*), national (*The Times*) and local (*Lynn Advertiser*), American (the *Michigan Daily*) and English (*The Manchester Guardian*), popular (*The Evening Standard*) and specialised (*The Times Literary Review*), from Scotland (*Inverness Courier*) to Australia (*West Australian*),[5] report on the discovery and publication as they relate to their own interests and readerships. Headlines declare the importance of the publication from divergent points of view, some of which seem comically sensationalist from a modern perspective.

THE TIMES

(October 10, 1936)

AMONG THE ENGLISH CLASSICS

The Autobiography of Margery Kempe

The Book of Margery Kempe, 1436. A Modern Version by W. Butler-Bowdon. With an
Introduction by R.W. Chambers. Cape. 10s. 6d.

The scholars must wait a little; we are given the new creature before the old. Lieutenant-Colonel
Butler-Bowdon's modernisation of his precious manuscript precedes Miss Hope Emily Allen's and
Professor Meech's edition of the text for the E.E.T.S. Whatever we may feel about this, the first
printed appearance of what Professor R.W. Chambers calls the "first extant biography in the English
tongue," and (of all wonders!) a spiritual autobiography, a travel-book and a domestic chronicle all in
one, to the original editor and presenter of it a unique formula of thanks must be registered. He
could have withheld it; it might have remained on his shelves without even reaching the museums,
far less the public mind of this generation; and a generation that knows not this fearless East Anglian
fifteenth-century mystic is poor-minded indeed.

Fig. 4. *The Times*

DAILY RECORD AND MAIL

(Glasgow, October 9, 1936)

WHEN MONKS WERE BOLD

WOMAN WHO TOLD PRELATE ABOUT THEM

Her Picture of England 500 years Ago

Fig. 5. *Daily Record and Mail*

LYNN ADVERTISER

(King's Lynn, January 4, 1935)

A REMARKABLE DOCUMENT

Light on Life in Early Lynn

THE STORY OF MARGERY KEMPE

Fig. 6. *Lynn Advertiser*

THE CHURCH OF ENGLAND NEWSPAPER
(Covent Garden, January 1, 1937)
THE BOOK WINDOW
The First English Autobiography and Other Personal Stories.

Fig. 7. *The Church of England Newspaper*

ISLINGTON & HOLLOWAY PRESS
(London, December 26, 1936)
ISLINGTON'S NEW BOOKS
'The Book of Margery Kempe.' A modern version by W. Butler-Bowdon.
(Central and West Libraries.)
In 1436, Margery Kempe, who had married "a worshipful burgess of Lynn" some forty years before, wrote what would nowadays be called her reminiscences.

Fig. 8. *Islington and Holloway Press*

CATHOLIC HERALD
(London, July 23, 1937)
Biography
DIRECTNESS OF MIND
The Book of Margery Kempe. A modern version by W. Butler-Bowdon. (Cape, 10s. 6d)
Reviewed by FRANCIS BURDETT
As all the world now knows, for owing to an accident this notice has been delayed, *The Book of Margery Kempe* has on many counts a quite unusual importance. She was the contemporary and friend, though how great a friend we do not know, of Julian of Norwich. Professor Chambers in his introduction tells us that Margery Kempe's book is the first extant biography in the English tongue.

Fig. 9. *Catholic Herald*

CHILDREN'S NEWSPAPER
(London, October 10, 1936)
MARGERY GOES A-WEEPING
An Indomitable Old Tramp
First Known Woman to Write Her Story in English
The Old Book on the Shelf

Fig. 10. *Children's Newspaper*

THE NEW YORK TIMES
(January 4, 1937) PRINTS LIFE TALE OF 1437 FEMINIST
Michigan University Unearths 'Book of Margery Kempe' From English Archives
ONCE DEFIED ARCHBISHOP
She was Tried for Heresy, but Piety, Tears or Sharp Tongue Got Her Off.

Fig. 11. *The New York Times*

THE MICHIGAN DAILY
(January 6, 1937)
Meech to Publish Manuscript of Pioneer English Biography

Fig. 12. *The Michigan Daily*

Here Kempe is a '1437 feminist' (*The New York Times*), 'a fifteenth century pioneer' (*Light*), an 'indomitable old tramp' (*Children's Newspaper*), the 'weeping woman of Lynn' possessed of a 'directness of mind' (*Catholic Herald*). Defying archbishops (*The New York Times*), reporting on bold monks (*Daily Record and Mail*), the 'woman in white' (*The Observer*) certainly seems to have got around ('The literary scene in Norway,' *New York Times Book Review*). Yet the stories behind the headlines have complexities beyond these attention-seeking words. The majority of Allen's clippings are taken from the years 1934, when the manuscript was discovered in Butler-Bowdon's house at Pleasington and identified by Allen for the Victoria and Albert Museum, through 1936, when the Butler-Bowdon modernised American edition was published and up to 1938, when the edition was being reviewed by newspapers and journals. As the *Times* put it, 'The scholars must wait a little; we are given the new creature before the old' (October 10, 1936, Fig. 4). In many ways this was to prove serendipitous. The publication of the scholarly edition by the Early English Text Society in England in 1940 during World War II was in itself remarkable, given printing restrictions and the fact that material had to travel across the Atlantic. Understandably, however, the modernised edition received more popular interest than the EETS edition was able or likely to.

Consistently, newspaper articles state that the Kempe manuscript is unusual even amongst medieval manuscripts. The discovery in the same year of the manuscript of Malory's *Morte D'Arthur* did not receive the same enthusiastic reception as Kempe's work, which was marked as a moment of particular significance. There are clearly differences between the two events. Primarily, of course, scholars knew about the Malory text before the Winchester manuscript was unearthed. Part of the interest in the Kempe text was its shock value, the recognition that the devout words known from sixteenth-century editions by Henry Pepwell and Wynkyn de Worde were only part of a larger work. The whole work, when it emerged, appeared to be a much baggier monster than the selections had led readers to believe. While, for scholars, the Winchester text provided fascinating new evidence about Malory, Caxton and the *Morte D'Arthur* in terms of its structure and Caxton's editorial policies, these were issues that did not catch the public imagination in the way that Kempe's text did.

Indeed, one of the reviews made a direct comparison between the Winchester Malory and the Kempe manuscript. While both were medieval manuscripts discovered when the material had only previously been known from later printed forms, the Kempe text was seen by *The Times* on September 30, 1936, as 'more unexpected and more important than the discovery of the "Morte d'Arthur" at Winchester.' Although the grounds for this perception are not directly articulated in the review of the Butler-Bowdon edition, it is possible to speculate as to what the major issues might have been. Most of these relate to the burgeoning sense of English as a national language and literature. While Malory's text was a romance, a fictional account of knights and courtly codes that was already nostalgic and fantastical by Malory's own time, Margery Kempe's text, on the other hand, was frequently trumpeted as a social document. For early reviewers one central significance of the text was its rôle in providing a window onto real life in the fifteenth century. Time after time, it is praised for the pictures of everyday life that it contributes, often compared with the Paston letters in terms of providing insight into the values and concerns of their time. It is this sense of 'realism' that is valued over the 'romance' of Malory's *Morte D'Arthur*.

Firmly connected to this is the appreciation of the text as not only a glimpse into fifteenth-century history but into *English* history. In this context the identification of the manuscript and the publication of the modernised edition occurred at a time when the notion of English as a discipline, as a national culture, was undergoing fundamental revaluation both in terms of secondary and tertiary education. As the pages of *Scrutiny* (1932) testify, English was being promoted in opposition to Classics, and the demand that English assert its own cultural heritage was being heard long and loud. From Matthew Arnold in the late nineteenth century to F. R. and Q. D. Leavis in the early twentieth century, the possibilities of a specifically English culture were being vigorously explored. Many of these arguments were being made in relation to modern culture rather than to the culture of earlier historical periods, and *The Book of Margery Kempe* would not have been at the forefront of any of the reformers' lists, yet the *Book* was, broadly speaking, consistent with the growing sense of the importance of English cultural values over imported ones. The foundation of the English Tripos at Cambridge marks a point in this development. With the establishment of a new course in 'English Literature, Life and Thought' in 1917, the employment of regular academic staff in English to replace the 'freelancers' after 1923, and at 'the end of the decade…the first group of students trained exclusively in English,' by 1930 English as a discipline was more firmly constituted.[6]

Prior to the establishment of *Scrutiny*, though, there had been the Newbolt Report of 1921, which reviewed the status and practice of English, amongst other aspects of the educational system. While in many ways *The Book of Margery Kempe* would not have been seen as an ideal text, from either Newbolt's or *Scrutiny's* perspectives, and this is not my argument, it is clear that the terms and contexts in which that text was discussed and the basis for its popularity were consistent with those that recur in the Newbolt report and in *Scrutiny*. For example, the former was at pains to argue that education should not be 'the presentation of lifeless facts' but should rather involve 'guidance in the acquiring of experience,' of which the 'most valuable for all purposes are those experiences of human relations which are gained by contact with human beings.' While these contacts might be made in a variety of places, including in the classroom between pupil and teacher, they could also occur 'through the personal records of action and experience known to us under the form of literature.'[7] Literature, thus conceived, is precisely that slice of life that *The Book of Margery Kempe* was seen to be, providing the kind of access to the human mind that the Report advocated.

> We must treat literature, not as language merely, not as an ingenious set of symbols, a superficial set of traditional gestures, but as the self-expression of great natures, the record and rekindling of spiritual experiences, and in daily life for every one of us the means by which we may, if we will, realise our own impressions and communicate them to our fellows.[8]

In this context, as R. W. Chambers wrote in his introduction to the Butler-Bowdon edition, on which most of the newspaper reviews are indirectly or directly based, *The Book of Margery Kempe* was indeed 'of the very greatest importance for the history of English literature.'[9] It is access to the life of Kempe, rather than its religious significance, which is seen as its main attraction in the reviews. So, through Kempe, we see a 'picture of England 500 years ago' (*Daily Record and Mail* 9 October 1936, Fig. 5), and the *Book* sheds 'light on early life in Lynn' (*Lynn Advertiser* 4 January 1935, Fig. 6). So the text is significant for providing access to human experience that is not only clearly identifiable as

English but is presented in specifically English terms as authentic. For *The Church of England Newspaper* (Fig. 7), this was a personal story, for the *Islington and Holloway Press*, the *Book* contained Kempe's 'reminiscences' (Fig. 8) This theme of authenticity is developed in the full review of Butler-Bowdon's edition by Francis Burdett in the *Catholic Herald* (23 July 1937, Fig. 9). Burdett was impressed by Kempe's 'frankness about herself' and saw in this fifteenth-century woman and text qualities lacking in Burdett's own time: 'What is so striking about her writing is the simple objectivity with which she narrates things and a directness of mind that is foreign to the way we live.'[10]

In this aspect the *Book* was like other select medieval texts that illustrated a time represented as inherently organic, wholesome and community based, much at odds with the perceived moral decay caused by the industrialism of the early twentieth century.[11] Derek Traversi, reviewing *Piers Plowman* in *Scrutiny* lamented this decline from "'a society closely connected to the land" where "honesty and active emotional responses came readily," to the desiccated life of a society ruled by the "deadening forces of modern industrialism,'"[12] in terms very similar to Burdett's. *The Book of Margery Kempe* was not then popular in spite of Kempe's 'boistowsnesse' or her awkwardness but precisely because of it and the authenticity or reality of the experiences it was seen to mark.

In addition, if literature is not 'language merely' for the Newbolt Report, then nevertheless advocates of English did focus on language as well, as a way of uniting England, and as the important primary medium through which all other skills and experiences were learned. Here, again, *The Book of Margery Kempe* met the mark. It arrived as a vernacular text with a robust and flamboyant use of language specifically identifiable as English. Newbolt cites France's proper respect for its own language as one that England had lacked: 'In France...this pride in the national language is strong and universal; the French artisan will often use his right to object that an expression "is not French."'[13] So for that bastion of English culture, the epitome of English standards, *The Times Literary Supplement*, this was not the least of *The Book of Margery Kempe*'s values, defined once again in terms of the favourite enemy, France: 'The happy fact that Norfolk was notorious for ignorance of French has given us an English fifteenth-century character whose speech and reaction to circumstances are as vivid and original as those of St. Joan herself.'[14]

A further way, then, in which the *Book* was nodal, performing and demonstrating those core values that the proponents of English were demanding, can be seen in the valuation of its commonsense or down-to-earth qualities. For the Newbolt Report this was a characteristic of the English people that literature and language should continue to represent and embody.

> The English are a nation with a genius for practical life, and the chief criticism directed, whether by parents or pupils, against our present system, is a practical one; it amounts, when coherently stated, to a charge that our education has for a long time past been too remote from life. We have come to the conclusion that this charge is supported by the evidence. However men may differ as to the relative importance of different objects in life, the majority are right in feeling that education should directly bear upon life, that no part of the process should be without a purpose intelligible to everyone concerned.[15]

Here, again, *The Book of Margery Kempe* fulfilled the important criteria, and we have another reason why it was significant to a wide range of newspapers and journals. *The Listener* specifically addressed this issue, pointing out that in this regard the *Book* was unlike many other medieval texts in that it had an appeal to a non-specialist audience: 'It is rarely that one can confidently recommend a medieval book to the general reader. *The Book of Margery Kempe*, however, is one of the exceptions. In the first place it is very easy to read in Mr Butler-Bowdon's excellent version; in the second it appeals to a variety of interests.'[16]

For two consecutive weeks, *The Observer* listed Butler-Bowdon's edition as one of the books most in demand in bookshops.[17] Here the timing of the edition, the nature of the text itself, and the fact that the modernisation came before the Middle English version coincided with an increase in the number of people who would be aware of it through newspaper reviews because of changes in the newspaper industry itself. So Raymond Williams identifies an 'expansion of readership and a concentration of ownership' between 1920 and 1947 in the industry.[18] For an industry changing its economic base to one dependent on advertising, an expansion of readership was critical. Moving from an educated intellectual élite to a larger audience meant providing material of a more generally accessible, less specialised nature. Happily, *The Book of Margery Kempe* arrived at a time ready for its robust Englishness and at a time that saw an increase in the general newspaper readership and a greater number of readers to hear about it. No wonder the Winchester Malory, with its antecedents in French romance, its length, its romance genre, did not cause the same stir, perhaps partly because of its at times gloomy portrayal of chivalry, of the decline from an Arthurian golden age.[19] Furthermore, precisely what made it interesting to scholars, the colophon at the end of section IV, rendered it irrelevant and inaccessible to the 'general reader,' that amorphous creature at whom the Butler-Bowdon edition was precisely pitched.

Alongside the crucial ways in which the Englishness of *The Book of Margery Kempe* marked it as a significant text, apart from the shock of the whole new *Book* that was much more than the parts had suggested, the text was also immediately identified as a new kind of text, as a first, although there seemed to be considerable confusion as to what it was the first of—autobiography or biography. *The Times* (Fig 4) and *The Catholic Herald* (Fig. 9) both quote the introductory essay by R. W. Chambers to the Cape edition that claims that this is 'the first extant biography in the English tongue,'[20] and many papers followed his view or directly quoted him to this effect.[21] Other articles insisted on the text's status as autobiography. This is, in fact, an ambiguity present in Chambers' own essay, as the second sentence of the essay from which the papers quote hedges its bets: 'The book is a biography, or autobiography.'[22] No doubt the ambiguities here reflected the uncertainty over the book's authorship and whether one could call a dictated book an autobiography.[23]

Related to the importance of the text as an authentic social document, as a life story whether biographical or autobiographical, is Kempe's gender. The word 'woman' is frequently used in the newspaper headlines of sixty years ago. Sometimes the significance of this is clear, as in the case of the *Daily Record and Mail*'s rather romantic 'Dark Ages' headlines: 'When monks were bold/woman who told prelate about them' (Fig. 5.) Here the word 'woman' emphasises the opposition between religious, naughty men and the devout, lay woman.

The Sphere (London, October 17, 1938) claims that the manuscript is 'The first English autobiography,' yet the *Children's Newspaper* qualifies the discovery of the manuscript by asserting Kempe to be 'The first known woman to write her story in English' (10 October 1936, Fig. 10)). Here the word woman quite clearly qualifies the claim, just as the phrase 'to write her own story' lacks the grandeur of the term 'autobiography' and sacrifices accuracy at the same time.

Kempe's aims are also frequently linked to her gender in these early reviews. *The New York Times* declares in its major headline that the *Book* is the 'tale of 1437 feminist' (Fig. 11), adding in the first paragraph that this is 'the pioneer militant feminist and evangelist who lived 500 hundred years ago.' This statement is only supported indirectly by quoting the scene in which Kempe describes herself as arguing against the Archbishop of York. On July 2, 1960, in Allen's obituary in *The New York Herald Tribune*, Kempe was again 'an early militant feminist,' yet it is interesting to note that these comments occur only in the American context, not the English.[24]

In neither case, nor in Allen's own discussion of feminism, is there any sense of the word 'feminist' being used disparagingly in these popular cultural contexts.

At most there is an amused sense of English eccentricity at work again, evident in papers on both sides of the Atlantic. This is clear in the English newspaper *The Observer*'s tongue-in-cheek account of the manuscript's discovery.

> It is strange that 'the first extant biography in the English tongue'—the Book of Margery Kempe—written in 1436–8, should have to wait five centuries for publication, but these things will happen in English country-house libraries. (4 October 1936)

The quaintness of the notion that fifteenth-century manuscripts commonly turn up in country-house libraries, almost willy-nilly, celebrates the sense of the English as an odd bunch of amateurs who acted peculiarly back in the fifteenth century and still don't know quite what treasures are lying around in their old houses. Like the Warden of Winchester's Tudor tapestry mat, unexpected treasures might be expected to turn up in England.

Yet here too there is a story behind the headlines that has only recently been clarified. The newspaper reviews consistently tell the story that the manuscript was sitting quietly on a shelf in Butler-Bowdon's library. 'The old book on the shelf' (Fig. 10) is seen as a 'library discovery' (*Lynn Advertiser*, October 9, 1936) that might have 'remained on his [Butler-Bowdon's] shelves without even reaching the museums, far less the public mind of this generation' (Fig. 4) were it not for the owner's labours. These accounts are entirely consistent with the owner's own memory of the situation as he described it for *The Times* on September 30, 1936, when his edition came out.

> The manuscript has lain in a bookshelf in the library of Pleasington Old Hall, Lancashire, next to a missal of 1340 in the rite of York, ever since I can remember. We used to look at it occasionally and sometimes visitors read a page or two of it.

This, after all, is not an unusual account. This is where one might expect to find a manuscript, and the account has a delightful air of well-heeled nonchalance about it. One can only envy Butler-Bowdon's guests getting their hands on the odd medieval manuscript during their sojourns at his old Georgian house.

Yet Hilton Kelliher and Sally Brown's *English Literary Manuscripts* has a tantalisingly different account stating that the 'autobiography of Margery Kempe turned up in a cupboard of household oddments, while the owner was searching for ping-pong balls.'[25] Until very recently the discrepancy between these two accounts was unexplained. Then Hilton Kelliher drew attention to a letter in Lynn Museum from Butler-Bowdon's son in 1970 that gave a rather less glamorous but, as Kelliher described it, 'charming' account of the discovery. In this version, according to Maurice Butler-Bowdon, the manuscript nearly ended

up on the bonfire on his father's instructions. One evening in 1934 the young
Butler-Bowdons were playing ping-pong when

> one of us trod on the Ping Pong ball and my father went to the cupboard to get out a
> replacement and it was soon apparent that he was having difficulty in finding either a ball or
> even the tube of balls. When our visitor (X) went over to assist the reason for the difficulty
> was obvious (we children knew it from experience). There was in there an entirely
> undisciplined clutter of smallish leather bound books. My father's retort to the hopingly
> helpful but unproductive visitor was 'Look X I am going to put this whole "_____" lot on
> the bonfire tomorrow and then we may be able to find ping pong balls and bats when we
> want them[.']To this X replied [']Willie, before you do anything so sudden may I ask an
> expert Z friend/acquaintance of mine who knows about these things to come and look
> through this cupboard, after all there may be something of real interest there which you may
> not at the moment realise[']....[26]

Fortunately the hospitable Butler-Bowdon senior did allow the expert to visit his
house, take the manuscript to the Victoria and Albert Museum, and subsequently
have it identified by visiting scholar Hope Allen.

The significance of these two different versions is minor in itself but does
provide a lighthearted example of the vagaries of historical discovery and the
discourses that develop around them. There seems little chance of ever telling
which of the two versions is closer to what actually happened. The son's story has
the attraction of having no vested interests while the father's is consistent with
the dignity of a lieutenant-colonel and an old Catholic family. Yet the son's is
written thirty-six years later and is part of the son's recollection of his family,
which could be unreliable. From a cultural materialist perspective, the later
account troubles the notion of cultural artefacts lovingly nurtured by genteel
benefactors and guarded for posterity. Here the transmission appears much more
haphazard and precarious, dependent on the vagaries and needs of the present,
such as the demands for bats and balls, in this case. The private account lacks the
dignity and gravitas of Butler-Bowdon's public declaration in *The Times* and attests
to the contingency of accounts of history, which has been a main tenet of
feminist historicism. The account you get depends on whose version it is, who is
telling the tale, a point made by Chaucer's Wife of Bath with reference to pictures
of lions and Aesop's *Fables*.

If the newspaper headlines conceal some stories or versions of the stories
behind the discovery of the Kempe manuscripts and its early editions, there are
also conspicuous absences from these headlines. Where is Hope Allen, the
identifier of the manuscript, specialist in medieval mysticism? Two other key
figures in the publications of *The Book of Margery Kempe* do appear, Sanford Meech

('Meech to publish manuscript of pioneer English biography,' *The Michigan Daily*, Fig. 12) and Colonel Butler-Bowdon, the manuscript's owner ('Colonel Bowden [sic] to Publish Text of the 14th-century Mystic's Autobiography,' *The New York Times*, August 24, 1937), but Allen, in whose collection these cuttings appear, is noticeably absent, raising serious questions about the nature and significance of female scholarship and the appreciation of it.

While Allen is absent from these public documents, her own position is evident from the Bryn Mawr College archives, where she puts her own point of view against these public records. The account of Monday, January 4, 1937, in *The New York Times* (Fig. 11), a piece of publicity for the University of Michigan, celebrates the activities of two of its staff members, Meech and Allen, who were then working on the *Middle English Dictionary* at Ann Arbor. Allen's annotations to the article indicate her sense of the inappropriateness of Michigan University claiming credit for an essentially independent exercise. Allen was, for most of her life, an independent scholar, surviving on her own personal income, derived from family interests in the Oneida Company and from occasional grants from bodies such as the American Council of Learned Societies. Only briefly was she aligned with, or employed by, a tertiary institution, and her independence is a significant element in her life as a scholar.

Allen's annotations speak volumes for her moral fastidiousness. Having identified error in Michigan's claiming credit for something in which it had only tangential responsibility, Allen then clarifies how the error occurred. Her annotations to the newspaper clipping indicate that the headlines were 'not written at Ann Arbor,' that 'the University of Michigan is not responsible for the headlines,' as 'the article alone was sent in by the reporter of the University…but the headlines were added in New York.'

Testament to much more personal concerns for Allen is the headline in the *Michigan Daily* two days later: 'Meech to publish manuscript of pioneer English biography.' The preceding chapters and Hirsh's biography cover the story of the EETS edition and what Allen called, in another context, the 'multiple objective and subjective forces at work' (BMC) that contributed to the problems surrounding the EETS edition. Here, in this private annotation of a public announcement, we see Allen suggest that the article, which does give her credit for identifying the manuscript and for preparing an introduction and notes was written 'by a student in the Michigan School of journalism and based on the N. Y. Times articles.' While Meech 'saw it before it came out (in my absence)' Allen ambivalently gives him the benefit of the doubt: 'he *may* not have seen the headlines' (my emphasis). The equivocations, the suspicion, the attempt to behave generously are all caught in the scrapbook record of newspaper clipping and handwritten commentary. The handwritten entry is all the more telling given that it is Allen talking to herself. In 1937 there is no suggestion that Allen intended her notes for public consumption. Getting the record straight is a matter of personal integrity and reassurance. Decades later the notes are also a disquieting voice of dissatisfaction, private annotations registering personal and scholarly marginalisation.[27]

Other headlines refer to ways in which the *Book* has been interpreted. *The New York Times* focuses on Kempe's battles with fifteenth-century authorities, although the paper seems unclear whether this was an isolated event or a series of events. On January 4, 1937, Kempe is described as having 'once defied archbishop,' whereas six months later 'she defied archbishops' in the plural. Kempe's resilience and her contempt for established authority that she believed to be acting improperly are emphasised in the newspaper accounts. Here we can see the beginning of a central debate in Kempe studies. Kempe's outspokenness with church authorities may seem to contradict the Christian doctrines the *Book* presents, yet most early critics, unlike recent critics, saw Kempe and the *Book* as fundamentally orthodox.

The New York Times Book Review, for example, discusses a collection of essays by Norwegian Sigrid Undset, describing Kempe's 'message...[as] wholly orthodox' (September 11, 1938). *The Church Times*, whilst acknowledging the prevalence of Lollardy in the late medieval period and its destabilising influence, sees Kempe as 'quite an orthodox person' (October 9, 1938). *The Observer* comments on the eccentricities evident within the Catholic religion in this period, but nevertheless describes the text as 'this orthodox autobiography' (October 11, 1936).

The orthodoxy of the *Book* was a crucial factor in Butler-Bowdon's enthusiasm for editing a modernised version of it himself. Fiercely defensive of the text and its protagonist, Butler-Bowdon had no doubts about Kempe's integrity. Butler-Bowdon's ownership of the manuscript, along with other religious artefacts,[28] is probably ascribable to the family's reputation as resiliently recusant, and Butler-Bowdon was certainly proud heir to a strong family history of Catholicism. In a slightly exasperated letter to Allen in January 1935, prior to the publication of his edition, Butler-Bowdon refers to the frequent requests for more information about Kempe, reserving particular scorn for modern Protestants.

The Church of England Clergy seem very anxious to connect her with their parish churches! It may not be out of place to remember that Margery was a Catholic, and that the

Reformation has taken place since she was alive, and also that the above mentioned Church
of England Clergy are the Lollards of the present day. (BMC)

Given the depth of Butler-Bowdon's feelings on religious issues, it is not
surprising that Allen registered the generosity of the colonel in allowing work to
be undertaken by two scholars not only foreigners—Meech and Allen being
American nationals—but also outside the faith. In a letter of December 1941
Allen wrote of wanting to bring Kempe 'to the cultivated general reader,' in
which context she states, 'It was generous of Colonel Butler-Bowdon to let this
work be done by non-Catholic scholars.' (BMC)

Allen herself was knowledgeable of a variety of religious matters. Her parents
had lived in the experimental Oneida community although she was born outside
of it, and she was primarily associated with research into medieval mysticism, in
particular, the works of Richard Rolle. She openly declared herself an agnostic,
and yet she too, like Butler-Bowdon, believed in the *Book*'s basic orthodoxy.[29]
Where the early twentieth century found conformity and orthodoxy, the late
twentieth century tended to find trangression.

Whatever the debates were and continue to be about *The Book of Margery
Kempe*, it is clear from these reviews and reports from the early days of Kempe
studies that the discovery of the manuscript of the complete text was a literary
event, regarded as a matter of significance to the literary and cultural world. In
these reports are the beginnings of a body of criticism about the *Book* and
Margery Kempe that was to evolve into Kempe studies. Some of the issues raised
in these early days persist in different forms. The auto/biography debate, for
example, can now be seen in the discussions about the level of Kempe's agency in
the text, about how much of the writing reflects Kempe's ideas, how much the
scribe's.[30] The initial interest in the gender issues of this first auto/biography in
English by a *woman* has become the focal point of most writing about the text in
secular literary and historical arenas and fundamental to discussions of the
religious dimensions of the text. In many ways emphases on the *Book* have
changed in the intervening seventy years since the manuscript's identification as
criticism has shifted from the public press to the academic, from the historian or
the religious commentator to the literary critic. Tracing the history of these
changes is a beginning of the project of a cultural materialist understanding of the
Book, and the varied contexts, productions, reproductions, receptions and
disseminations through which the *Book* exists.

A final anecdote concerning the discovery of that other 1934 manuscript
serves to illustrate the importance of material such as Allen's scrapbooks to the
cultural materialist. Oakeshott's account of the identification of this manuscript

describes it too as 'the result of a fortunate series of accidents.'[31] On the lookout for original fifteenth- and sixteenth-century bindings, Oakeshott found Malory, and from this makes an interesting point about the nature of scholarship, using the language, vocabulary, and imagery prevalent in Oakeshott's own time.

> We are told that Saul the son of Kish went out to seek his father's asses and found a kingdom. The fate of the literary detective is comparable only in that, if he finds anything at all, he will find something different from that for which he is looking. It is seldom a kingdom. It is often a mare's nest. The asses almost always prove elusive.[32]

Looking for ping-pong balls, perhaps, Butler-Bowdon found a manuscript. Researching the *Ancren Riwle* and Richard Rolle, Hope Allen found Margery Kempe. Looking for material for Allen's projected second EETS volume, we find the scrapbooks of reviews. While Bryn Mawr College Archives reveal no neat, complete drafts of articles just waiting to be published, they are more than a mare's nest. In the collection of reviews, in the letters and notes are fragments towards a fuller picture of the history of the Kempe manuscript, its discovery and its initial reception. The inclusion of these issues in the field of Kempe studies is a stage in the development of a cultural materialist history of the *Book* and discourses about it, which, in turn, shed light on the nature of contemporary scholarship.

Notes

1. W. F. Oakeshott, 'The Finding of the Manuscript,' *Essays on Malory*, ed. J. A. W. Bennett (Oxford: Clarendon Press, 1963), p. 2. As a rather sad aside, Oakeshott's account reveals that for M. R. James 1934 was clearly not a good year, as he missed the chance of involvement with both of these remarkable manuscript discoveries. If Allen's account that James was asked but declined to see the Kempe text is correct, and Oakeshott's account is too, then his remarks have an added poignancy in suggesting that James missed out in identifying two significant medieval manuscripts: 'That great scholar, M. R. James, had the Malory in his hands more than once before I saw it; it was a piece of singular good fortune for me that its importance did not happen to strike him' (p. 6).

2. Ibid., p. 5.

3. The scrapbooks are in box five of the BMC collection.

4. The extracts reproduced here are simply a selection from Allen's collection. The criteria used in selecting them included diversity in terms of newspaper type, location and readership, and the use of headlines. My selection does not distort the collection but does represent the most dramatic material in the collection.

5. These brief reports are not shown here but the *Inverness Courier* report was October 6, 1936, and the *West Australian* May 15, 1937.

6. Francis Mulhern, *The Moment of Scrutiny* (London: New Left Books, 1979), p. 22.
7. 'The Teaching of English in England,' or the Newbolt Report (1921), named after the chair of the committee, Sir Harry Newbolt, appointed by the Board of Education in 1919. *The Nineteenth-Century History of English Studies*, ed. Alan Bacon (Aldershot: Ashgate, 1998), p. 298.
8. Ibid., 307.
9. *The Book of Margery Kempe 1436: A Modern Version by W. Butler-Bowdon*, introduction by R. W. Chambers (London: Jonathan Cape, 1936), p. 1.
10. This correlation of women with the *Book* and the unproblematic reading of the latter as simply factual have been consistent trends in Kempe criticism. They fail to see the text within what Barbara Newman called 'the parameters of literary composition,' *From Virile Woman to WomanChrist: Studies in Medieval Religion and Literature* (Philadelphia: University of Pennsylvania Press, 1995), p.15. Allen, at the beginning of Kempe criticism, was firmly convinced of the need to see Kempe's text in terms of its rhetorical strategies: 'It must never be forgotten that hers was a work of active propaganda' (BMC).
11. This also seems to be reminiscent of the nineteenth-century romanticisation of the Middle Ages.
12. Francis Mulhern, 1979, p. 56.
13. Alan Bacon, ed., 1988, p. 308.
14. *TLS*, October 10, 1936.
15. Alan Bacon, 1988, p. 297.
16. *The Listener*, October 28, 1938.
17. *The Observer*, October 25 and November 1, 1936.
18. Raymond Williams, *The Long Revolution* (Harmondsworth: Penguin Books Ltd., 1973), p. 229.
19. I am grateful to David Matthews for suggestions on this issue.
20. R. W. Chambers, introduction to *The Book of Margery Kempe 1436: A Modern Version by W. Butler-Bowdon*, 1936, p. xvi.
21. See, for example, Fig. 9.
22. R. W. Chambers, 1936, p. xv.
23. In the first sentence of Butler-Bowdon's note in the modernised edition, he refers to the *Book* as autobiography. A letter from Butler-Bowdon's son Maurice gives a sense of how Butler-Bowdon junior saw the matter: 'I think it would be more right to refer to the Book as an autobiography because, after all, she dictated it to a priest to write down just as, nowadays, one would dictate to a secretary.' Letter dated January 30, 1970, held in Lynn Museum, King's Lynn, Norfolk.
24. The term 'feminist' is not now usually applied to Kempe. Verena E. Neuburger, *Margery Kempe: A Study in Early English Feminism* (Berne: Peter Lang, 1994) is an exception.
25. Hilton Kelliher and Sally Brown, *English Literary Manuscripts* (London: The British Library Board, 1986), p. 5. I am grateful to Jane O'Sullivan for alerting me to this discrepancy and to correspondence with Hilton Kelliher and his subsequent publication of his clarifying article 'The Rediscovery of Margery Kempe: A Footnote,' *The British Library Journal* 1997, 23: 2, pp. 259–63.
26. I have quoted from the original letter dated Friday, January 10, 1970, from Maurice Butler-Bowdon to a Mrs 'Luck,' which seems to be Maurice's error for 'Tuck'. This letter is held by

Lynn Museum, King's Lynn, Norfolk. Hilton Kelliher quotes the main passages in his article (1997).

27. Letters between Wake and Allen in the Northamptonshire Record Office also indicate that Chambers' contribution to the modernised edition of the *Book* took place without notice to Allen. This adds a further dimension to Allen's sense of being sidelined from the first publications of the manuscript she had identified and for which in many ways she felt responsible. The watchdog finds herself bitten.

28. This is drawn to public attention in Allen's letter to *The Times*, December 27, 1934.

29. Ibid.

30. See, for example, the competing perspectives of John C. Hirsh's 'Author and Scribe in *The Book of Margery Kempe*' in *Medium Ævum*, 1975, pp. 145–150, where he argues that 'the second scribe, no less than Margery, should be regarded as the author of *The Book of Margery Kempe* (p. 150), and Carolyn E. Whitson's Ph. D. thesis *The Anatomy of Conflict: Gender and the Strategies of Agency in "The Book of Margery Kempe,"* University of California, Santa Cruz, 1994.

31. W. F. Oakeshott, 1963, p. 1.

32. Ibid., p. 6.

Chapter 5

Institutionalising Margery Kempe:
The Scholarly Debates, 1934–2004

> When a club cricketer scores a hundred we congratulate him and leave it at that; we do not criticize him for not being good enough to play for England.
> —Martin Thornton, *Margery Kempe: An Example in the English Pastoral Tradition*

In the twenty-first century, in a little over seventy years, Margery Kempe has gone from being a little-known writer of some spiritual understandings to the subject of a number of full-length academic studies and collections of essays and a proliferating number of postgraduate theses.[1] There have been both major changes and continuities in the criticism about Kempe and the *Book* in this period of time, and throughout there have been tensions and arguments about the status of Kempe and the *Book* as objects of study as the epigraph delightfully suggests. Adopting a chronological survey, one can see some clear differences across the short history of Kempe criticism. For example, initial reaction emphasised the authenticity of the *Book*, reading it as an account of fifteenth-century life, while contemporary criticism is much more likely to identify transgressive factors in the book and person of Kempe.

Yet while differences are identifiable across this seventy-year period, there are also themes and issues that recur throughout the history of the *Book*'s publication. In addressing these similarities and differences it is useful to re-examine Stanley Fish's notion of 'interpretive communities'[2] as a way of thinking not only about textual interpretation but also about its location within historical contexts. For Fish, thinking about interpretive communities solved the problem of locating meaning either within the text (in which case why was there so much disagreement about any one text?) or in the individual reader (in which case why was there so much agreement?). Interpretive communities constitute

> a point of view or way of organizing experience that shared individuals in the sense that its
> assumed distinctions, categories of understanding, and stipulations or relevance and
> irrelevance were the content of the consciousness of community members who were
> therefore no longer individuals, but embedded in the community's enterprise, community
> property.[3]

Fish usefully explains why there is neither one interpretation per text nor one per reader in an essentially deconstructive turn and produces a theory of interpretation that has at its heart the notion of change. If members of the community share an 'interpretive disposition,'[4] then by working on a particular object they also change what is said about that object and the parameters of what it is possible to say about it.

Fish's notion of interpretive communities, then, gives us two ways of thinking about Kempe criticism. First, it is possible to review the criticism and to identify particular interpretive schools from which it arises. Without being overly schematic, we can then see that there are groupings around specific concerns or positions. Within Kempe criticism two of the most obvious of these would have to be a religious community or orientation and a feminist orientation. There is also, of course, a sub-set that is the intersection of these two groupings. Broadly speaking, in Kempe criticism it can be said that the early dominance of a religious orientation has given way to a feminist orientation. Where the former focussed on the spiritual meanings of the *Book*, the latter tends to centre on issues of gender. This, in turn, raises issues of who constitutes the communities from which these differing discourses emerge.

Less obviously, there are also differences between what we might call a historical and a literary orientation. Whereas the early stages of the former examined *The Book of Margery Kempe* for what it could reveal about life in late fourteenth- and fifteenth-century Lynn, the focus of the latter has been on the text as narrative, the rôle of the author, and, increasingly, on the strategies of the narrator. Criticism on Kempe over the last ten years is more literary than historical, more feminist than religious. Once these broad changes have been noted, it then remains to ask how these changes have occurred and what differences there are in Kempe criticism over the seventy years. The rest of this chapter examines three different sites within Kempe criticism, 'Englishness,' 'authenticity,' and 'gender,' both in terms of historical changes since the 1940s and in terms of the communities from which the criticism arises, taking into consideration the changes in the constitution of those communities.

One characteristic of the earliest Kempe criticism is that it treated the *Book* as a social document, replete with evidence of life in medieval England. One of the first article-length pieces on Kempe occurred in the *Downside Review*, a journal that went on to develop a long history of interest in Kempe. Attributed to 'A Benedictine of Stanbrook,' this 1938 piece was a response to the publication of Butler-Bowdon's modernized version and signalled its interest immediately in the opening paragraphs. While the article focussed especially on what can be learnt about the practices of the Eucharist, more generally the *Book* was seen to 'throw a vivid light on everyday life in England five centuries ago, and in particular on the religious faith and practice of the author herself and her contemporaries.' From what is learnt in reading the book, the reviewer then confidently asserts that Kempe is 'no morning star of the Reformation. On the contrary, she is as aggressively orthodox a Roman Catholic as ever lived.'[5]

In the same year, in the secular journal *History: The Quarterly Journal of the Historical Association*, D. L. Douie made much the same point about the *Book*'s 'particular value for the reconstruction of the ordinary social life of the fifteenth-century.' Where the specific interest for the Benedictine was the religious domain, for the historically minded Douie the work was 'particularly useful for the light it sheds on the lives and interests of the citizen-class, which through the development of trade was increasing so rapidly in wealth and importance.'[6] Broad agreement concerning the historical significance of the document sits alongside the divergent interests that historicity might serve. For Douie, too, there is information here concerning devotional practices of the time, but the personal aspects of Kempe's mysticism and the book are 'the most uninteresting part of it.'[7] With this, and the reference to the Wife of Bath as Chaucer's fictional counterpart to Kempe, many of the themes of Kempe criticism over the ensuing decades are established.

Evidence of one other major theme exists in the commentaries of two other writers in this first period of Kempe criticism. Before the publication of any Kempe text, Herbert Thurston first wrote of Kempe as 'Margery the Astonishing,' describing the manuscript as 'an intensely personal document' but also emphasising its 'freshness and vigour of language.'[8] For the Rev. Sir John R. O'Connell, again in *The Downside Review*, in 1937, this was developed into one of the most important features of the work. For these scholars, like the newspaper reviewers, it is not just what the book tells us about history that makes it important but that it tells us about English history. Furthermore, it does so in an identifiably English way, invoking notions of linear development and progress in the evolution of English studies. From this kind of thinking comes a clear identification with England, the English language, and all things English.

This book is of supreme importance because it is the first conscious and deliberate autobiography in the English tongue and not less because it is written with a vigour and vividness which marks a notable advance in the common use of the vernacular in the development of the English language. This book shows a definite progress on the road of the growth of English which came to something akin to perfection a century later in the English prose works of St Thomas More.[9]

Martin Thornton was working a similar theme of Englishness more than twenty years later when, with a particular interest in the English school of spirituality, he focussed, in the subtitle of his book, on Kempe as 'An Example in the English Pastoral Tradition.'[10] From him came the charming analogy, quintessentially English, with which this chapter began.[11] To compare Kempe with other mystics, he argued was unfair. Margery Kempe would have been a 'first-class parishioner,' and her value lies in reminding us of 'real solid English religion.'[12] For *The Times Literary Supplement* Kempe's Englishness was enough to guarantee her status, 'her book...is an English classic, while Juliana's—is a book of English devotions only.'[13] For Thornton, though, her Englishness entailed setting odious comparisons with Julian of Norwich aside:

Julian is a mystic, Margery is not. Julian disturbs, rouses, and terrifies us: Margery gently teaches and guides. Julian is the mystical Professor: Margery is the Sunday-school teacher and comparative values apart, it is the latter whom most of us need.[14]

The analogies with cricket, the local church organisation, and the university specifically address the issues of hierarchy within religious debates over Kempe, but they are also entirely evocative of England and Englishness, for which many commentators were prepared to forgive Kempe much: 'She may be a little over-emotional, she may be an "enthusiast," she may be a pest; but she is as English as a Norfolk hedgerow.'[15] No less identifiably English, one might argue, is this kind of criticism.

More specifically, this particular comment says as much about a particular kind of construction of Englishness as it does about Kempe's England in the fifteenth century. Invoked here are images of rural England, characteristic of nineteenth-century images of medieval England. The appeal here is to an idealised earlier England, a warmer, more organic society as opposed to the industrialised England of the late nineteenth and early twentieth century, a land of eccentric but simple souls. Medievalism here is substituting 'the paternal benevolence of manor and guild for the harshness of factory and offering the clean air and open fields of the medieval past in place of the blackening skies of England.'[16] These ideas all come to mind in Thornton's imagery with the allusions to village life, the parish, country fields, and hedges. What could be more English than hedgerows?

Yet if this imagery invokes England, which England? At the heart of Thornton's writing are markers of his own time and space. The hedgerows he invokes demarcate one person's property from another, and were not a feature of Kempe's own time. They became so after the enclosure acts. Thornton's imagery is as rich in allusions to his own time and its specific constructions of medievalism as it is of fifteenth-century England. The scholarly institutional-isation of Kempe is also part of the institutionalisation of England and Englishness in cultural terms. Emphasising the eccentric—mad dogs and English women—produces an affectionate homage to a rich history and culture that appears unthreatening, always already there, familiar and homely, to be celebrated rather than deplored, loved rather than feared.

All of these interests, these ways of reflecting on or inflecting the *Book*, necessarily represent the values of the interpretive community from which they come. There were religious differences between these early critics. Thurston was an ordained Catholic priest, Thornton a priest of the Oratory of the Good Shepherd, W. R. Inge, another early commentator, was Dean of St Paul's. T. W. Coleman, again involved in the debates about early English mysticism, directly addressed these religious differences when he suggested that he could bring a fresh perspective to the field as 'the first free Churchman to issue a book on this subject.'[17] Nonetheless, there are clearly convergences of interests from these well-educated religious men, whose own lives and those of their ancestors were sufficiently significant in English history to merit recording in *Who Was Who*. There are 'categories of understanding,' as Fish put it,[18] which serve to demarcate the parameters of discussion within which debate occurs. For the first three decades, then, of Kempe criticism, those in the possession of the knowledge, skills, and experience to deal with *The Book of Margery Kempe* concentrated on nationalism and spiritualism that were necessarily their major concerns.

In many ways, as Hirsh pointed out,[19] the tendency to focus on the *Book*'s importance as a document of social history, as descriptive of an earlier England, had begun with Hope Allen and her description of a presumed desire on the part of Kempe 'to set everything down as it first happened.'[20] For Allen this perception was clearly linked with the sense that while Kempe's work needed to be put into the context of continental mysticism,[21] it was nevertheless part of 'a history of medieval feminine piety in England.'[22]

Yet not only was the subject matter particularly English, as Allen saw it, but so too was the *Book*'s publication by EETS in 1940 characteristically English: 'Your nation and your nation alone would have produced this book in the circumstances in which it came out.'[23] Allen articulates one example of the way in which medieval studies has been influenced by 'specific ideological or local, nationalistic or religious, political or personal interests of those who have shaped them.'[24] Like medievalists before and after her,[25] Allen saw this as part of a way of consciously relating the present to the past, of relating her own work on medieval subjects to political events going on around her. In 1940 she wrote of the importance of collaboration on a putative edition of the *Ancren Riwle* in terms that stressed its political as much as its scholarly significance. For her it was 'one of the prime sources of Anglo-Saxon civilisation—one of the things that makes England what it is in this war today.' Not only was it symptomatic and formative of English values for the American Allen, but she hoped that it would also have future power and influence in terms of 'propaganda value' (BMC). The study and criticism of *The Book of Margery Kempe* is then inextricably connected to the specific history of criticism in English and the development of a national consciousness, particularly in the early stages, given the social and political background of the war years. It is, however, also characterised by the tradition of critics' concern with the contemporary as well as the past. As Donald Howard put it in his exploration of what a new 'Fourth Medievalism' might look like, this involves acknowledging that if the medieval period 'is a "distant mirror," we will see in it, as in all mirrors, a selective, reversed, and distorted image in which we cannot help but see ourselves.'[26]

So, one strand of early criticism saw Margery Kempe as indisputably English and concentrated on the importance of national identity in a period of crisis, and one amorphous group of critics firmly aligned itself with varieties of explicitly religious communities. The notion that *The Book of Margery Kempe* was a social document also gave rise to the idea that Margery Kempe herself could be extrapolated from the text as an identifiable, determinable figure. Here Allen triggered another debate, this time concerning Kempe's state of mind, her normality or abnormality, her authenticity or the lack thereof.

Allen's notes in the EETS text on the speculative connections between Kempe and other continental women mystics connected Kempe, for Allen, with her social and historical context. E. I. Watkin, however, saw this as an attack on Kempe through calling into question her originality. Allen's notes, he felt, 'lose no opportunity of exhibiting her as the rival and copyist of other women visionaries.'[27] Writing 'In Defence of Margery Kempe' against the charge of fanaticism, Watkin placed his faith, literally, in reading Kempe through the book and arriving at his opinion of her trustworthiness.

My intention is frankly to undertake her defence, not simply in the hope of obtaining the heavenly reward promised, she tells us, to her champions (!) but because after careful study of her life both in the modernised version and in the original text I am convinced that she loved God and her neighbour with a genuine, deep and wholehearted love. And this after all is the sum and substance of sanctity.[28]

Leonard Bacon, three years later, also wrote of Kempe's sincerity and of the book as a 'first hand report.' He confirmed Kempe's account with his own evidence from 'a delightful nun,' 'that being a bride of Christ was not all roses.'[29] For Watkin and Bacon, originality and immediacy are the hallmarks of authenticity.

These responses are characteristic of the first wave of Kempe criticism, which, as both Roberta Bux Bosse and Hirsh argue,[30] was generally more enthusiastic than critical. Yet if Kempe's book and the extrapolation of Kempe from the *Book* were part of a definitional move in terms of Englishness, then she also served as a negative definitional moment in debates about mysticism. She and the *Book* become a negative example. While W. R. Inge found Julian of Norwich's *Revelations of Divine Love* a 'most beautiful gem of medieval literature' ('I know no more charming book than hers,'),[31] Kempe suffered by comparison, and Inge excluded her from his book, *Mysticism in Religion*.

> I have not troubled my readers with Margery Kempe, unearthed in 1934....This hysterical young woman calls herself a poor creature, and a poor creature I am afraid she was. She is obviously proud of the 'boisterous' roarings and sobbing which made her a nuisance to her neighbours. She never quite rings true.[32]

Giving the impression that he himself would have been just as happy had Kempe remained lost to history, Inge saw Kempe as not only the standard by which Julian's worthiness can be appreciated but as the standard against which true mysticism can be measured.

> mysterious sights, sounds and smells, 'boisterous' fits of weeping, cataleptic trances, stigmata, apparitions....These results of unrestrained emotionalism belong rather to psychology and psychopathy than to religion.[33]

Kempe then demonstrates what religion and mysticism are by embodying what they are not. Positioned as the excluded other from Inge's account of mysticism, Kempe functions in an anthropological sense as dirt, which, as Mary Douglas wrote, 'offends against order. Eliminating it is not a negative movement, but a positive effort to organise the environment.'[34] The exclusion of Margery Kempe from the mystical canon provides that against which the canon can be defined.

Reinforcements in the Kempe cause arrived in 1948 when Katherine Cholmeley increased the stakes by describing her, in the subtitle of her book *Margery Kempe*, as 'Genius and Mystic.' Here, bowing to the decrees of Pope Urban VIII, Chomeley acknowledged that only the Pope had the 'power and authority to pronounce as to whom rightly belong the Character and Title of Saint or Blessed.'[35] Yet Butler-Bowdon's preface to the book argued that Cholmeley was qualified to assess whether or not Kempe was genuine because both Kempe and Cholmeley shared the characteristics of being Catholic and female: 'For these reasons she can understand Margery's outlook, and her fear of delusion, as others, however deeply versed in mysticism, in general, might not.'[36]

These altercations over the status of Kempe's authenticity and sincerity, the 'is she/isn't she' debate, continued to be a feature of Kempe criticism. Up until the late 1970s and 1980s articles still signalled their intentions to line up on one side or another of the line, most seeking to rehabilitate Kempe.[37] While arguing that a reassessment of Kempe's reputation was necessary, Roberta Bux Bosse was also one of the first to suggest that the 'either or debates' were missing the point: 'The truth lies somewhere between these extremes; Margery is neither an egomaniac nor a genius.'[38]

Bosse also continued to argue the connection between Kempe and the *Book* in the sense that the former could be read off from the later: '[the *Book*'s] fascination is due to the vividness with which it depicts her personality,'[39] but abrogated the rights, which Cholmeley had attributed to the Pope, to judge the claims of Kempe's authenticity, and assigned them to an even-higher authority, the final transcendental signifier: 'As to the quality of Margery's mystical revelations only God could judge accurately.'[40] Bosse began to re-evaluate the way the *Book* had been treated, to consider issues of genre, to argue that 'the real hero of Margery's treatise is not Margery herself, but Christ.'[41] While William Provost still worked within a binary opposition of the *Book* as either 'fantasy or even fraud, rather than an early autobiography, a serious self-portrayal of a fascinating human being,' he too argued that the real question was 'not whether Margery's work is worth reading but how or as what to read it.'[42]

At this point it is worth raising the vexed issue of naming. If 'a woman's problematic relation to society is signified by her name, and her name is part of a woman's problem,'[43] then nowhere is this more true than in and around *The Book of Margery Kempe*. Sue Ellen Holbrook describes the case in relation to the text itself: 'Within the narrative of Book 1, her name does appear in direct address: fifteen times as Margery by friendly figures speaking to her and once as the daughter of John Brunham, Mayor of Lynn.' Elsewhere, consistently, she is '"this creature," accompanied by the third-person singular pronouns,'[44] clearly designating the significance of her relationship with the Creator, God.

For critics, the practice of naming the figure in and of the text also serves to illustrate the nature of their relationship with her. The early friendly critical figures tend to opt for first-name terms, as demonstrated, from the examples given above, by the practice of the Benedictine, Thurston, Thornton, and Provost, in contrast with the more formal approach of her detractors, such as Inge. In recent years the business of naming has also been raised explicitly. Lynn Staley Johnson first suggested, in a footnote to an article, that a distinction be made between 'Margery, the subject, and Kempe, her author,' as part of developing interest in *The Book of Margery Kempe* as text, as fiction, and as narrative strategy—an interest that culminated in Staley's later book and the concept of the *Book* as 'dissenting fiction.'[45] Cheryl Glenn then further complexified the move to distinguish personae with her arguments concerning controlling author and fictional strategies: 'Margery-the-actual-(flesh-and-blood)-author creates Margery-the-implied-author (a persona that dictates to the scribe) who creates Margery-the-character ("this creature"). Hence, Margery Kempe is preserved.'[46] Complicated as these equivocations are they nevertheless tell us about shifts and consistencies in Kempe debates. The interest in distinguishing between Margerys and Kempes suggests an unease with the tendency to unproblematically read off 'author' from text. Both Staley and Glenn concern themselves with the text as rhetoric and construct rather than 'fact,' or 'history.' In this sense they distance themselves from early criticism intent on the *Book* as fifteenth-century verisimilitude. Yet both also, inevitably, tend then to write more of Margery than Kempe and are thus part of the process through which she becomes familiar in two distinct senses.

First, we know and hear more about Margery Kempe now than we used to. She has become a familiar figure in critical debates and in various different kinds of anthologies. Second, we tend to be accustomed to seeing her referred to as 'Margery,' which carries its own weight in the process of familiarisation. It also individualises and personalises her, sometimes patronises her, and renders her less alien. Through creating a sense of familiarity and knowability, this practice removes the reader further from the experience of reading the *Book* itself, and the significance of all these tendencies needs to be evaluated. In concentrating on 'textuality' rather than fact, on literature rather than history, there remain issues for feminist criticism. It might be useful to make distinctions between 'author' and subject in relation to Margery Kempe, but the justification originally used by Staley Johnson is problematic. Critics do 'commonly distinguish between Will, the layabout, and Langland, the author, or between Geoffrey and the poet Chaucer,'[47] but the dimensions of gender and genre need to be factored in here. The necessity for the categories of 'Geoffrey,' and 'Will,' was driven by the need to distinguish between author and persona, and there never was a tradition or tendency for the critic to forget his or her own position relative to the author sufficiently to lapse into first name familiarity. The necessity for a category of 'Margery' may arise from similar reasons, but there are significant differences. First, *The Book of Margery Kempe* is not fictional or literary in the ways that *The Canterbury Tales* or *Piers Plowman* is. Second, there is a critical tradition that already sees Margery Kempe, the 'author,' as 'Margery,' and this cannot be ignored or written over in terms of the gendered implications. Third, and external to the text itself, the politics and sexual politics of naming press upon these practices. Who has the right or power to use first names is a highly charged issue and carries significant implications. The practice of calling women writers by their first names, while referring to male writers by their surname or full name, indicates attitudes about the relative level of respect meted out to a writer dependent on their gender. In this sense while the frequent use of Kempe's first name in critical contexts might be driven by quite different aims in 1934 and now, it is arguable that some of the effects are the same.

In the last twenty years there has been a resurgence in Kempe studies, through the influence of feminism, following the enthusiasm of the 1930s and 1940s and the identification of the manuscript, and a decline of interest in the 1950s and 1960s. Given a chronological perspective, there seems a clear shift in the kinds of interpretive communities producing scholarly discussion of *The Book of Margery Kempe*. While the first commentators could be characterised, generally, as likely to be male, religious, educated and 'establishment,' the constituents of the second wave were rather more heterogenous. These critics might be either male or female, religious or secular, but they were most likely to be professional intellectuals—academics.

Behind this shift can be seen changes in the number of women participating in education, and higher education in particular, and changes in the nature of higher education towards a notion of general or mass education. Just prior to Allen's own enrolment in the class of 1902, women's enrolments generally in the USA went from 21 percent in 1870 to 34 percent in 1900. Female students at the University of Chicago correspondingly went up from 24 percent in 1892 to 52 percent in 1902. In England in the same period the expansion in the number of female students was also experienced as "'an unexpected revolution.'"[48] Given this kind of numerical increase one might wonder why this was not more strongly reflected in the kinds of criticism occurring.

There are different kinds of answers to this question. While there were certainly more women undergoing some kind of higher education, that did not entail that the kind of education they received was equal to or valued equally with that experienced by men. As we saw in chapter 2 of this book, the nature of women's education was still very much a controversial issue in the USA and UK in the early twentieth century. Indeed, while Cambridge University admitted women as early as 1869, it did not permit them to attend lectures and did not allow them to undergo the same kind of undergraduate program as men until 1947, although another English university, the University of London, did significantly earlier in 1878.[49]

The increase in numbers of female undergraduates was then significantly slower than the increase in the number of women participants in higher education. Following this was another very slow increase in the number of women hired to teach and research in institutions of higher education. Norman Cantor describes the position of medieval historian Eileen Power among the small group of women 'who were the product of the first great generation of British feminism' which emerged in the 1920s and 1930s.[50] Cantor argues for the significance of Power even within this special group as she was specifically focussed on women's history and a married woman.[51] He describes the climate that militated against such successful participation by women in academia as well as family life.

> Sexual autonomy was perhaps a necessary defence for this generation of women medievalists making their way in a profession that was intrinsically hostile to them and accepted them begrudgingly and essentially required of them that they work within the prevailing ethos of a male-dominated medievalist world.[52]

It is in an understanding of the 'prevailing ethos' that a second kind of answer can be given to the question of why when Kempe studies flickered in the 1950s and 1960s, it flared up again from the 1970s onwards, and why when it did so it took quite different orientations. This is also partly the question of why 'it was really the generation of the 1970s and 1980s' that saw a burgeoning in the development of women's studies, women's history, and an interest in the specifics of gender in literary studies for which Cantor saw Power as being an early model,[53] rather than Power's own generation. For Dale Spender, it was through the phenomenon of the 1960s' consciousness-raising, through discussions between women, that a sense of the importance of women's experience developed more strongly and more popularly. As a sharing of experiences revealed to individual women in the 1960s that their experiences were often not isolated or deviant but common, so too questions were raised about previous women's experiences:

were there women who had felt like this in the past, how many of them were there, what had they said?…Why were women of the present cut off from women of the past and how was this achieved?[54]

To these kinds of questions then came answers: 'Fundamental to patriarchy is the invisibility of women, the unreal nature of women's experience, the absence of women as a force to be reckoned with.'[55] From these kinds of answers came commitments to rectify these invisibilities, to record the experiences, and to people the absences. Just as the EETS's aim was to make accurate editions of Middle English texts avaliable for further scholarship and promulgation, so the establishment of publishing companies such as Virago and The Women's Press Limited provided texts by, for, and about women for gender-based analysis. So, as political feminists would argue, while an increase in the number of women in higher education was certainly necessary to the development of a scholarship interested in gender, it was not sufficient without a political understanding of the contexts in which gender operates and is constructed.

The growth of feminist criticism shifted the ways in which Kempe was discussed and the context in which discussion occurred. The knowledge of *The Book of Margery Kempe* also interacted with feminist concerns.

> Adding women's writings to the canon, finding a tradition of women's writing, exploring differences between men's and women's writing, studying representations of femininity in texts by women as well as by men, locating stories of "strong" women, locating medieval women at all—for all these transformative activities in the academy, *The Book of Margery Kempe* does great service.[56]

In this context, William Provost's work is indicative of such a shift in the focus of Kempe studies. His essay occurs in a collection entitled *Medieval Women Writers*[57] and was part of an increasing emphasis on Kempe's gender as an explicitly significant factor. Mary Beth Rose's *Women in the Middle Ages and the Renaissance*[58] also reflected new clusters of interest and concerns. Here an essay on Kempe sits alongside an essay on women in the Italian inquisition, one on Shakespeare's heroines, and another on the Countess of Pembroke. The connections between these diverse topics are gender and the early modern period, a connection that now seems self-evident. Janel M. Mueller's essay in this collection directly addresses the history of Kempe criticism, acknowledging the tendency of Kempe debates so far to cling 'to either/or thinking.'[59] The shift away from treating the book as social history with the second wave of Kempe criticism towards a more specifically literary approach, concerned with form, is also signalled in the title of Mueller's essay, as is the interest in gender, 'Autobiography of a new "Creatur": Female Spirituality, Selfhood, and

Authorship in *The Book of Margery Kempe*.' Here, the increased interest in issues of gender is aligned with interest in form and genre and with subjectivity. These conjunctions have remained the focus of the last twenty years,[60] and in these debates it is gender that is the central organising issue.

More recently, class, gender, and history are being brought together. Among the most compatible accounts of Kempe criticism with cultural materialism is Sarah Beckwith's work. Highlighting the 'persistent doubt as to her authenticity,' Beckwith asked why there has 'been a debate about Kempe at all, and why [has it] been staged so obsessively in this way.'[61] In trying to answer these questions Beckwith argued that '*The Book of Margery Kempe* foregrounds the very conditions of subjectivity itself.'[62] Beckwith's arguments are firmly grounded in marxist and materialist accounts of identity and agency provided by writers such as Bakhtin. Her emphasis is also characterised by an intense interest in subjectivity and identity within literary criticism derived from the influence of French psychoanalytical theorists.

Yet beyond, around, and in between much of this discussion on Kempe, authorship and narrativity, there still lurks an obsession with Kempe as a personality identifiable from the book. In this sense, the connections between early Kempe criticism that emanated from specifically religious contexts and contemporary feminist criticism are closer to the surface than might be thought initially. 'Modern criticism,' argued Michel Foucault, 'in its desire to "recover" the author from a work, employs devices strongly reminiscent of Christian exegesis when it wished to prove the value of a text by ascertaining the holiness of its author.'[63] The search for subjectivity in *The Book of Margery Kempe* is not necessarily different in kind from the debates over Kempe's authenticity, and here feminist criticism does not escape the problematics of these debates.

The search for women in history, for 'strong' women, for medieval women, confronts particular problems with *The Book of Margery Kempe*, problems that are specific to it, yet that are also symptomatic of some general problems in feminist criticism. What is known about Kempe external to the *Book* would do more than cover the back of a postage stamp and occupies several notes and an eighteen-page appendix in the EETS edition, but it is nevertheless not extensive. There are simply not many records of events in Kempe's life outside of the *Book* itself. In that context the best historical work, such as Atkinson's, Gallyon's, and Goodman's,[64] has used detailed knowledge of local history to build up a picture of Lynn that is representative rather than particular to Kempe.

Furthermore, Lochrie is right to suggest that Kempe cannot be claimed as a feminist nor as a champion of women and to 'find Kempe's behavior undesirable as a feminist practice.'[65] Yet the tendency remains to take *The Book of Margery Kempe*, extrapolate Kempe from it, and then render her in terms meaningful to the values of contemporary criticism. So she becomes a 'social critic,' an 'anti-social virus in the body politic,' a woman who 'transgresses the nexus of medieval taboos governing the female body,'[66] in ways that distort the basic principle of the book, which is to demonstrate its orthodoxy and the worth of Kempe as a follower of Christ.

The elision of the book with Kempe has also resulted in a tendency to take the book at face value, to treat it as if it were factual or a realist text. Taking Kempe at the book's word has been a consistent theme throughout seventy years of criticism. If in the earliest stages the debate oscillated between the poles of sincerity and fakery, criticism in the last twenty years has shifted the terms but not the basic assumptions about how to read the book. Lochrie's *Margery Kempe and Translations of the Flesh* still often invokes a scatological, wilfully subversive woman. The debate has shifted from orthodoxy to transgression but the facticity of the book is still implicitly or explicitly assumed. Both approaches assume that the *Book* is realist in mode and pay little attention to it as project and propaganda, as literary and rhetorical.

Furthermore, the emphasis on gender in recent studies of the medieval period provokes the question from Allen J. Frantzen, 'Are women enough?'[67] While the need to see Kempe as other than demonised, fraudulent, hysterical, insincere, or simply wrong is understandable and part of the feminist revision of history, there are often tensions between these approaches and the need for an understanding of historical differences. The emphasis on Kempe as a person, as a woman in a particularly patriarchal period of history, has partly arisen from feminist interest in the book. As in early feminist criticism on other literary topics, such as the claims that Shakespeare, Dickens, and Milton can all really be seen as 'feminist,' there has been a strong tendency to recuperate Kempe for the modern feminist canon.

While feminists have rightly wanted to re-interpret *The Book of Margery Kempe* as other than hysterical or spiritually inferior, the reclamation of Kempe has involved an essentialism that has been criticised within other areas of literary criticism. To see the book as accurately representing events in Kempe's life and to read from these descriptions Kempe as a radical, battling against senior male clergy, raises certain important questions. If Kempe were as outspoken as the book describes her as being, if her contemporaries thought her as subversive as some modern criticism likes to see her, how did she escape punishment, given that in 1401 the priest of her own parish, William Sawtre, was burnt at the stake for heresy? Historical evidence suggests that Lynn, Kempe's hometown, was associated with Lollardy and hereticism, while only forty kilometres away in Norwich 'at least sixty men and women were tried for heresy by the episcopal court between 1428 and 1431,'[68] that is, within Kempe's lifetime. Why Kempe escaped if she were perceived as subversive is a question of history that needs to be asked and answered.[69]

It is tempting, given the interest of current literary theories in transgression and subversion, to rescue Kempe from debates on mysticism that see her at worst as neurotic and hysterical, at best as a second-rate mystic in comparison with her historical contemporary and geographical neighbour Julian of Norwich, and to claim her as a radical female figure, explicitly tackling the dominant masculinist assumptions of her day. However, Sheila Delany's warnings about recent valorisations of Christine de Pisan are relevant to feminist critics investigating women from earlier historical periods. Locating herself in a tradition of feminist scholarship through her use of Virginia Woolf's project of finding 'mothers to think back through,' Delany argues for the necessity of remembering the politics of a materialist feminist perspective. Recognising the necessity of 'rehabilitating women whose work has been neglected,' Delany nevertheless argues that 'the very effort to reconstitute a full understanding of women's participation in cultural history can result in a skewed perception of individual contributions and of history at large.'[70] Specifically in relation to Kempe, Sarah Beckwith raised similar concerns:

> In much contemporary social, including feminist, theory, agency is either reified in the typically essentializing accounts of the authenticity of female experience unrelated and unconstructed by society or by convention or by techniques of representation and their institutional matrices, or conversely it is made to disappear altogether as the mere passive victim of social structure.[71]

A further dimension is added to the problem of adequately discussing the life of someone like Kempe when we acknowledge the arguments of post-structuralist theorists against essentialist accounts of human subjectivity without relinquishing the gains that feminists have begun to make in demanding that women, in the past and in the present, be accorded the same respect as functioning agents that men have been accorded. It is necessary to negotiate a path between the scylla of liberal humanist criticism, which seeks to uncover the 'facts' of Kempe's life from scant material evidence, and the charybdis of a post-structuralism that argues that 'the field is *theoretically*, not merely empirically unknowable.'[72] We cannot stand by Kempe's side, but we can investigate what evidence there is to elaborate our understandings of the *Book*, as Hawthorn suggested.

if the reader cannot become a contemporary of the author, and if a reader's own situation necessarily impacts upon his or her reading of a literary work, then readers should perhaps start to see if they cannot marshal the resources of their own time and situation in the most productive manner.[73]

At the broader level of feminist theory this involves acknowledging issues canvassed in the thought-provoking but critically neglected work by Elizabeth Fox-Genovese on feminism and individualism. Taking the slogan 'the personal is political,' Fox-Genovese argues that 'the real lesson of the middle-class feminism of the 1960s and 1970s is that the personal is social' but that 'in a crazy reversal, the politicization of the personal becomes the personalization of the political, in which individual women justify their own successes and arbitrary choices in the name of sisterhood.'[74] The significance of this for Kempe studies is clear. It is not sufficient to argue one way or the other concerning Kempe's spiritual authenticity—the final arbiter of which could only be the ultimate transcendental signifier—but nor is it possible to find in Kempe a radical 'mother to think back through.' The reclamation of women for history involves the need to reinvestigate that history rather than merely elevate a few individual women whose records we are fortunate enough to have.

Much explicitly religious criticism sought to recuperate Kempe for its own cause while some denied that her credentials were sufficient for her to join the club. Feminist criticism rightly tried to redescribe the agendas or criteria according to which Kempe's work was assessed and discussed but nevertheless remained caught up in traditional parameters. To invoke another sporting metaphor, 'Rather than disrupting the individualistic values by which the mainstream canon has been created, feminist critics sometimes merely replaced a male First Eleven with a female one.'[75] Now, however, we are entering a period where feminist analysis is re-engaging with history, is attempting to understand women of the past in ways that acknowledge the importance and influence of contemporary concerns, without re-writing those women in the image of modern feminist values.[76] An analysis of criticism will also, from a cultural materialist perspective, always involve an analysis of the period in which it was written, and more needs to be done in this area. By reframing the cruxes of scholarly debate in terms of the cultural conditions of the time, we not only understand more about values of the recent past but about our own. For many medieval critics, perhaps more than for other historicists, this has always involved considering the past in relation to the present. As well as rethinking the value of Kempe and her text, we also need to understand the history of Kempe criticism, her journeys from certifiability[77] to institutionalisation within medieval scholarship. Part of this institutionalisation can be seen through interrogating the appearance of Kempe in anthologies and editions, through charting her passage from selections of devotional material to teaching text.

Notes

1. John Skinner gives anecdotal evidence of the increase in the number of theses, *The Book of Margery Kempe* (New York: Image Books, 1998), p. 10. *The Cambridge Companion to Medieval Women's Writing*, eds. Carolyn Dinshaw and David Wallace (Cambridge: Cambridge University Press, 2003) discusses its current canonical status.

2. Stanley Fish first developed this concept in *Is There a Text in This Class?* (Cambridge, Massachusetts: Harvard University Press, 1980), and then reworked it in *Doing What Comes Naturally* (Oxford: Clarendon Press, 1989), especially chapter 7. Kathleen Ashley uses this idea to address Kempe's first audiences, 'Historicising Margery: *The Book of Margery Kempe* as Social Text,' *Journal of Medieval and Early Modern Studies* 28.2 Spring 1998, 371–88.

3. Stanley Fish, 1989, p. 141.

4. Ibid., p. 303.

5. A Benedictine of Stanbrook, 'Margery Kempe and the Holy Eucharist,' *The Downside Review* 56, 1938, p. 468.

6. D. L. Douie's review of Butler-Bowdon's edition, *History: The Quarterly Journal of the Historical Association*, ns. XXII, p. 70.

7. Ibid, p. 72.

8. Thurston first published 'Margery the Astonishing: A Fifteenth-Century English Mystic' in *The Month*, November 1936, and then republished the article, with minor alterations, in *Surprising Mystics* (Chicago: Henry Regnery Co., 1955). These quotations can be found in the 1936 version on p. 446, in the 1955 version on p. 27.

9. Rev. Sir John R. O'Connell, "Mistress Margery Kempe of Lynn," *Downside Review* 1937, 55 p. 176. O'Connell had published a life of Thomas More two years before in 1935.

10. Martin Thornton, *Margery Kempe: An Example in the English Pastoral Tradition* (London: Talbot Press, 1960).

11. Ibid., p. 3.

12. Ibid., pp. 3 & 85.

13. *The Times Literary Supplement*, October 10, 1936.

14. Thornton, op. cit., p. 76.

15. Ibid., p. 54.

16. Alice Chandler, *A Dream of Order: The Medieval Ideal in Nineteenth-Century English Literature* (London: RKP, 1971), p. 12.

17. T. W. Coleman, *English Mystics of the Fourteenth Century* (London: Epworth Press, 1938), p. 7.

18. Stanley Fish, 1989, p. 141.

19. John C. Hirsh, 'Margery Kempe,' ed. A. S. G. Edwards, *Middle English Prose: A Critical Guide to Major Authors and Genres* (New Brunswick, New Jersey: Rutgers University Press, 1984), pp. 109–20.

20. Hope Emily Allen, letter to *The Times*, Thursday, December 27, 1934.

21. This was to be one of the main arguments of the projected EETS volume two, which Allen was working on until shortly before her death in 1960 but which was never completed. Bryn Mawr Archives contain most of Allen's notes and papers towards this volume, but there is not enough to be able to reconstruct a satisfactory shape and design for the volume.

22. MS Engl. Misc. c. 484.

23. MS English. Letters d. 217.

24. R. Howard Bloch & Stephen G. Nichols, *Medievalism and the Modernist Temper* (Baltimore: The Johns Hopkins University Press, 1996), p. 4.

25. See, for example, Maxine Berg's work on medieval economic historian Eileen Power, who brought the 'present into the past' in relating her international political beliefs to her medieval studies (*A Woman in History: Eileen Power 1889–1940*, Cambridge: Cambridge University Press, 1996, p. 262 & passim). For neither Power nor Allen was the past a dead object of study but rather a source of illumination and relevance for the present.

26. Howard is quoted in James M. Dean and Christian K. Zacher, *The Idea of Medieval Literature: New Essays on Chaucer and Medieval Culture in Honor of Donald R. Howard* (Newark: University of Delaware Press, 1992). The reference is to Barbara Tuchman's *A Distant Mirror: The Calamitous Fourteenth Century* (New York: Knopf, 1978). Pierre Macherey's use of the mirror image as a way of understanding the relationship between literature and society is also helpful, *A Theory of Literary Production* (London: Routledge and Kegan Paul, 1978).

27. E. I. Watkin, 'In Defence of Margery Kempe,' *Downside Review* July 1941, LXIX, p. 118. This article was republished as a chapter with the same title, with some minor alterations, in his *Poets and Mystics* (New York: Books for Libraries Press, 1953).

28. Ibid., p. 244.

29. Leonard Bacon, review of the Butler-Bowdon edition, *Saturday Review of Literature*, November 4, 1944, p. 12.

30. Roberta Bux Bosse, 'Margery Kempe's Tarnished Reputation: A Reassessment,' *Fourteenth Century English Mystics Newsletter*, March 1979, pp. 9–19; John C. Hirsh, 'Margery Kempe,' 1984.

31. Very Rev. W. R. Inge, *Mysticism in Religion* (London: Hutchinson and Co. Ltd., 1947), p. 124. Paul Crook's article 'W. R. Inge and Cultural Crisis 1899–1920' in *The Journal of Religious History* 16:4, December 1991, pp. 410–432 provides fascinating information about Inge's background and goes some way to providing a picture of the context in which critical discourses are developed, which is necessary to a full cultural materialist account of the criticism of this period.

32. Inge, op. cit., pp. 10–11.

33. Ibid., p. 13.

34. Mary Douglas, *Purity and Danger: An Analysis of the Concepts of Pollution and Taboo* (London: Ark Paperbacks, 1984), p. 2. See also Jonathan Dollimore's 'The Dominant and the Deviant: A Violent Dialectic,' *Futures for English*, ed. C. McCabe (Manchester: Manchester University Press, 1988).

35. Katherine Cholmeley, *Margery Kempe: Genius and Mystic* (London: The Catholic Book Club, 1948), p. vi.

36. Ibid., p. vii.

37. See, for example, Roberta Bux Bosse 'Margery Kempe's Tarnished Reputation: A Reassessment,' and Drew E. Hinderer's "On Rehabilitating Margery Kempe,' *Studia Mystica* 5.3, Fall 1982, pp. 27–43.

38. Bosse, ibid., p. 9.

39. Ibid.

40. Ibid., p. 10.

41. Ibid., p. 15.

42. William Provost, 'The English Religious Enthusiast: Margery Kempe,' ed. Katharina M. Wilson, *Medieval Women Writers* (Athens: University of Georgia Press, 1984), p. 298.

43. Margaret Anne Doody, *Frances Burney: The Life in the Works*, (New Brunswick: Rutgers University Press, 1988), p. 6. I am grateful to Dianne Osland for this reference.

44. Sue Ellen Holbrook, '"About Her": Margery Kempe's Book of Feeling and Working,' James M. Dean and Christian K. Zacher, *The Idea of Medieval Literature*, p. 267.

45. Lynn Staley Johnson, 'Margery Kempe: Social Critic,' *Journal of Medieval and Renaissance Studies* 22: 2, Spring 1992, p. 159; Lynn Staley, *Margery Kempe's Dissenting Fictions* (Pennsylvania: University of Pennsylvania Press, 1994).

46. Cheryl Glenn, 'Author, Audience, and Autobiography: Rhetorical Technique in *The Book of Margery Kempe*,' *College English*, 54:15, September 1992, p. 545.

47. Lynn Staley Johnson, 'Margery Kempe: Social Critic,' p. 159.

48. This reference and the figures are taken from *Storming the Tower: Women in the Academic World*, ed. Suzanne Stiver Lie and Virginia E. O'Leary (London: Kogan Page Ltd., 1990), p. 19. See also Carol Dyhouse, *No Distinction of Sex: Women in British Universities, 1870–1939* (London: UCL Press, 1995).

49. Ibid., p. 33.

50. Norman Cantor, *Inventing the Middle Ages: The Lives, Works, and Ideas of the Great Medievalists of the Twentieth Century* (New York: William Morrow and Co. Inc., 1991), p. 389.

51. Power was married to another academic, M. M. Postan.

52. Ibid. While I agree with Cantor's account of these female dons' marital status, it is also possible to wonder whether the adage that what a successful career woman needs is a wife was not already being appreciated at this stage. If it was hard to be successful without the help of a wife, it was probably also hard to be successful and a wife. The dons that Cantor cites are Helen Maud Cam, Beryl Smalley, Dorothy Whitelock and Maude V. Clarke (p. 389).

53. Ibid.

54. Dale Spender, *Women of Ideas and What Men Have Done to Them: From Aphra Behn to Adrienne Rich* (London: Routledge and Kegan Paul, 1982), pp. 3 & 4.

55. Ibid., p. 11.

56. Sue Ellen Holbrook, '"About Her,"' p. 279.

57. Wilson, op. cit., p. 298.

58. Mary Beth Rose, ed., *Women in the Middle Ages and the Renaissance* (Syracuse, New York: Syracuse University Press, 1986).

59. Janel M. Mueller, 'Autobiography of a New "Creatur": Female Sprituality, Selfhood, and Authorship in *The Book of Margery Kempe*,' Mary Beth Rose, ed. *Women in the Middle Ages and the Renaissance*, p. 160.

60. See, for example, Sarah Beckwith's work, 'A Very Material Mysticism: The Medieval Mysticism of Margery Kempe,' ed. D. Aers, *Medieval Literature: Criticism, Ideology and History* (Brighton: Harvester Press, 1986), 'Problems of Authority in Late Medieval English Mysticism: Language, Agency, and Authority in *The Book of Margery Kempe*,' *Exemplaria* 4.1 March 1992, pp. 171–99, and *Christ's Body: Identity, Culture and Society in Late Medieval Writings* (London: Routledge, 1993); Karma Lochrie's work, '*The Book of Margery Kempe:* the Marginal Woman's Quest for Literary Authority,' *Journal of Medieval and Renaissance Studies*, 16.1, Spring 1986, pp. 33–55, 'The Language of Transgression: Body, Flesh, and Word in Mystical Discourse,' ed. Allen J. Frantzen, *Speaking Two Languages: Traditional Disciplines and Contemporary Theory in Medieval Studies* (Albany: State University of New York Press, 1991), and *Margery Kempe and Translations of the Flesh* (Philadelphia: University of Pennsylvania Press, 1991); and Carolyn Elizabeth Whitson, *The Anatomy of Conflict: Gender and Strategies of Agency in "The Book of Margery Kempe,"* Ph.D. thesis, University of California, Santa Cruz, 1994.

61. Beckwith, 1992, p. 177.

62. Ibid., p. 179.

63. Michel Foucault, *Language, Counter-Memory, Practice,* ed. Donald F. Bouchard, trs. Donald F. Bouchard & Sherry Simon (Ithaca: Cornell University Press, 1977), p. 127.

64. Clarissa Atkinson, *Mystic and Pilgrim: "The Book of Margery Kempe" and the World of Margery Kempe* (Ithaca: Cornell University Press, 1983); Margaret Gallyon, *Margery Kempe of Lynn and Medieval England* (Norwich: The Canterbury Press, 1995); Anthony Goodman, '*The Book of Margery Kempe' and Her World* (London: Longman, 2002).

65. Karma Lochrie, *Margery Kempe and Translations of the Flesh,* p. 9.

66. Lynn Staley Johnson, 'Margery Kempe: Social Critic,' 1992; Antony E. Goodman, 'The Piety of John Brunham's Daughter of Lynn,' *Medieval Women,* ed. D. Baker (Oxford: Blackwell, 1978); Karma Lochrie, *Margery Kempe and Translations of the Flesh,* 1991, p. 7.

67. Allen J. Frantzen, 'When Women Aren't Enough,' *Speculum* 68, 1993, pp. 445–471. While the title of the article is provocative, it nevertheless makes important points about the uses to which gender has been put by both 'traditional and innovative scholarship,' p. 445.

68. Clarissa W. Atkinson, *Mystic and Pilgrim,* p. 104.

69. I return to this in chapter 7.

70. Sheila Delany, '"Mothers to Think Back Through": Who Are They? The Ambiguous Example of Christine de Pizan,' ed. Laurie A. Finke & Martin B. Shichtman, *Medieval Texts & Contemporary Readers* (Ithaca: Cornell University Press, 1987), pp. 178 & 179.

71. Sarah Beckwith, 1992, p. 198.

72. Gayatri Chakravorty Spivak's introduction to Jacques Derrida's *Of Grammatology* (London: The Johns Hopkins University Press, 1976), p. xix.

73. Jeremy Hawthorn, *Cunning Passages: New Historicism, Cultural Materialism and Marxism in Contemporary Literary Debate* (London: Arnold, 1990), p. 80.

74. Elizabeth Fox-Genovese, *Feminism Without Illusions: A Critique of Individualism* (Chapel Hill: University of North Carolina Press, 1991), pp. 28 & 32.

75. Mary Eagleton, *Feminist Literary Theory: A Reader* (Oxford: Blackwell, 1990), pp. 3–4.

76. In terms of Kempe studies specifically, the work of Sarah Beckwith, Sue Ellen Holbrook, Lynn Staley (Johnson) and Carolyn Whitson is representative. For discussions of the uses of history more generally from a feminist perspective, see Joan Wallach Scott, *Gender and the*

Politics of History (New York: Columbia University Press, 1988). For accounts of intellectuals and scholars, see Maxine Berg, *A Woman in History: Eileen Power 1889–1940* (Cambridge: Cambridge University Press, 1996), and her chapter on Power, ed. Edward Shils and Carmen Blacker, *Cambridge Women: Twelve Portraits* (Cambridge: Cambridge University Press, 1996), and John C. Hirsh, *Hope Emily Allen* (1988).

77. Roy Porter discussed Kempe in terms that focussed on her personal insanity even if he did argue that her madness had a method in it, 'Margery Kempe and the Meaning of Madness,' *History Today*, 38, February 1988, pp. 39–44.

Chapter 6

Reproducing the Texts:
The Books of Margery Kempe

> The physical format of the book…provides a situational context for any actual reading of it.
>
> —Paul Eggert, *Editing in Australia*

On many different occasions Margery Kempe expressed her concern about her appearance and indicated her awareness of both what she meant by it and how it will be interpreted by others. From the start of Book 1, the reader is made aware of the specific purposes Kempe had in mind when, before her religious conversion, she dressed her body to influence others: 'Hir clokys also wer daggyd and leyd wyth dyuers colowrs be-twen þe daggys þit schuld be þe mor staryng to mennys syght and hir-self þe mor ben worshepd' (9:15–18). ('Her clothes were slashed and laid with different colours between the slashes so that they would be more arresting and herself more respected.') On two different occasions Kempe also noted the ostentatious dress of others as demonstrating a concern with impressing other people and as a mark of pride, where there ought to be a concern with humility and obedience to God. Kempe attacks the Bishop of Winchester's men for being 'al-to-raggyd and al-to-daggyd' (109:11), and the conversion of her son is indicated by the change in both behaviour and appearance: 'For a-for-tyme hys clothys wer al daggyd and hys langage al uantye; now he weryd no daggys, and hys dalyawns was ful of vertu' (223:31–34). ('For before his clothes were ostentatious, and his language very trivial; later he didn't wear fancy clothes and his conversation was virtuous.')

Throughout her book, Kempe maintains a consistent understanding that what she wears contributes to how others interpret her, that physical appearance is closely connected to the production and reception of meanings. It is simply that the range of meanings, and her intentions, have changed from these early pages. Her initial anxiety about wearing white, as God has asked her to, for example, is that this will be interpreted by others as an act of hypocrisy, as indeed it is: 'yf I go arayd on oþer maner þan oþer chast women don, I drede þat þe pepyl wyl slawndyr me' (32:19–20). ('if I go about dressed differently from other chaste women, I fear that people will criticise me.') For a married women and mother of fourteen children to wear white contravenes the common understanding of the symbol of virginity.

On other occasions, the book testifies to the ways that this representationalist aspect of clothes is manipulated by others with whom Kempe comes into contact precisely to alter the meanings she has in the world, in particular situational contexts. The point of abusing Kempe through cutting her gown off short, so that 'it cam but lytil be-nethyn hir kne' (62:15–16), is specifically to affect how others see her, so that 'sche xuld ben holdyn a fool and þe pepyl xuld not makyn of hir ne han hir in reputacyon' (62:17–18). The disturbing thing about Kempe's account of this incident is that she is rendered helpless to the prejudices of her companions and loses control over the meanings generated about her as she well understands.

On yet another occasion, Kempe reasserts her ability, if not to determine, at least to affect what it is that is said about her and what it will mean. It is a telling incident in the book and is intimately connected with an understanding of Kempe's relations with the hierarchy of the Church, a point reconsidered in my next chapter. Challenged by her enemy, the Mayor of Leicester, as to why she, as wife and mother, is wearing white, and confronted with the curious charge that her doing so is indicative of her anti-social intention of stealing away other men's wives, Kempe refuses to answer these accusations because the Mayor is 'not worthy' (116:16) of a direct explanation from her. In this public context, however, Kempe does not leave the explanation ungiven but significantly gives the reasons, not to the secular authority that demands it but to the religious authorities that will then be able to sanction her account and substantiate the alternative interpretation that she wishes to have known. She specifically selects her audience to ensure the safety of her message.

> "ser, I wil tellyn it to þes worthy clerkys wyth good wil be þe maner of confessyon. Avyse hem ȝyf þei wyl telle it ȝow." Than þe clerkys preyd þe Meyr to gon down fro hem wyth þe oþer pepyl. And, whan þei weryn gon, sche kneyld on hir knes be-for þe Abbot, and þe Den of Leycetyr, and a Frer Prechowr, a worschipful clerke, and telde þes iij clerkys how owr Lord be reuelacyon warnyd hir and bad hir weryn white clothys er sche cam at Ierusalem. (116:16–25)

> "sir, I will tell it to these worthy scholars with good will, by way of confession. Let them consider if they will tell you." Then the scholars asked the mayor to go away from them

with the others. And when they had gone, she knelt down before the Abbot and the Dean of Leicester, and a Friar-Preacher (a worshipful scholar) and told these three scholars how our Lord by revelation had warned her and bade her wear white before she arrived in Jerusalem.

Through controlling to whom she speaks and what form or genre that speech takes, Kempe can encourage a particular kind of interpretation.

Sue Ellen Holbrook has argued that the production of *The Book of Margery Kempe* and its interpretations are something that the book self-consciously considers. She suggests that there were in fact other kinds of books that could have been produced, that these might well have had different effects, and explores what the implications of this might have been for Kempe herself. Through focussing on the 'making' of the *Book*, Holbrook interestingly directs attention to the situational contexts in which it operated and which determined the shape that it came to have.[1] In this chapter I want to consider the guises in which *The Book of Margery Kempe* has appeared since the identification of the manuscript in 1934 and the intentions and receptions of those guises. Through thinking about the physical and literary formats of the *Book*, we can identify the relationships between intention, appearance, and reception and broaden our understandings of the range of meanings that it has come to have. We can also reconsider what it is we actually mean by 'The Book of Margery Kempe.' In doing this I also hope to be moving towards what Raymond Williams envisaged in his call for a critical theory that is more than a theory of consumption and that sees literature 'as a practice in society.'[2] This process involves acknowledging the 'ineluctably economic'[3] dimensions of texts. It 'also directs us to consider the human motives and interactions which texts involve at every stage of their production, transmission and consumption. It alerts us to the rôles of institutions and their own complex structures in affecting the forms of social discourse, past and present.'[4]

Sue Ellen Holbrook and Karma Lochrie have each discussed the first forms of *The Book of Margery Kempe* as it was known in the sixteenth century through the annotators' comments on the Salthouse manuscript and in the Wynkyn de Worde extracts, published by him in 1501 and then anthologised with other spiritual writings by Henry Pepwell in 1521.[5] Their analyses of these first versions go a long way toward exploring the kinds of material the first readers of Kempe's work encountered, the contexts in which they existed, and the kinds of readings to which they might have given rise. The de Worde edition then can be seen in its specific contexts, as one of the quartos that 'fit the hand well and were comparatively inexpensive to produce, thus suiting both user and maker.' Here, '*A shorte treatyse of contemplaycon* becomes in appearance what the excerptor had made the *BMK* into: a manual of practical mysticism.'[6] By extending the kinds of analysis provided by Lochrie and Holbrook to the modern versions of the text, we can extend our awareness of 'how our own readings are constructed by the circumstances of publication and transmission of texts and by our own cultural investment[s].'[7]

The first version to which twentieth-century readers were exposed was an edition based on the sixteenth-century anthology, a reprint of Pepwell's edition, by Edmund Gardner in 1910. After the identification of the manuscript in 1934, these selections from the full text were measured specifically against contemporary twentieth-century values. In evaluating the merits of the manuscript against the extracts, Meech described the latter thus:

> In conclusion, the prints of de Worde and Pepwell are of very slight value in establishing original readings of the *Book of Margery Kempe*. They are of some interest in showing that some elements of the *Book* seemed to experienced printers of the sixteenth century to be worth publishing. These elements were, from a modern literary point of view, the less spectacular and human ones." (xlviii)

The key phrase here, of course, is 'modern literary...view.' Meech's comments were made at the beginning of World War II, at a time of great crisis, whose dimensions could hardly be more spectacular and human.

Meech is right to suggest that the selections seem less satisfactory, measured against the whole text, from a modern perspective. It should also be added that in this particular case they seem less satisfactory, specifically in relation to gender. They exclude some of the information about fifteenth-century England, and a particular woman's account of this, which is precisely what has made the book so fascinating to two generations of feminist scholars. The de Worde and Pepwell selections were aimed at those interested in mystical and spiritual matters. As Holbrook put it, the extractor 'left behind all that is radical, enthusiastic, feminist, particular, potentially heretical and historical.'[8] The full text achieved a much wider appeal, from historians, feminists, and religious scholars. The quite different situational contexts produce very different editions for different audiences, which, in turn, promote quite different kinds of discussion.

The EETS edition was the first to make the full text available to twentieth-century scholars, as of course it made many other medieval texts available. Comparing this publication with the Salthouse manuscript does, however, suggest two things. First, that while the EETS text may have had a reputation for unevenness in the nature of the material it published and in the quality of the scholarship around it,[9] the Meech and Allen edition seems admirably accurate.

Second, however accurate it is, the EETS edition is still a very different physical entity to the manuscript, and this has implications for the relationships between reader and text. In particular, the flatness of the printed version renders the interpolations of the sixteenth-century readers, the marginal annotations, much less an intrinsic part of the whole reading experience than they are on the manuscript. Here, the different hands and the different inks, though faded and obscure, signal their differences from each other and from the Salthouse hand in which the text is written. They also insistently alert the reader to the presence of other readers gone before. But the EETS edition was not the first appearance of the full text in the twentieth century.

What, then, are we to understand from the first twentieth-century version of the full manuscript, Colonel Butler-Bowdon's? In 1936, prior to the publication of the EETS scholarly printing of the text of the manuscript, Colonel Butler-Bowdon produced for Jonathan Cape *The Book of Margery Kempe 1436: A Modern Version*. Referring to the forthcoming EETS edition, as 'a literal copy of the manuscript,' designed to 'meet the demands of experts and scholars,' Butler-Bowdon made the point that 'the archaic spelling and meanings preclude its easy perusal by the ordinary reader.'[10] It is with a general audience in mind that he has produced his own modern version, updating the spelling and replacing words whose meanings he regarded as difficult or obsolete.

Fascinatingly, however, in this 1936 edition, he also reversed the process undertaken by de Worde and Pepwell. At the end of his volume he provided a list of the selections made by de Worde, and gave their corresponding pages in his own edition. In an appendix, he listed the thirty pages removed from the main body of the text, for which he explained his reasons. In a letter to Hope Allen he also wrote that he hoped she would

> approve of this version of 'Margery.' To avoid the ordinary reader becoming wearied with too much mysticism I have resorted to an appendix. This contains mystical chapters complete—a better method to my mind than scrappy cutting—so that the more studious reader can take the book easily in sequence if he wants to. (BMC)

He accounted for this editorial intervention, like Meech, in relation to his sense of contemporary audience.

> Except to those particularly interested in it, the great amount of mystical matter would probably prove wearisome. Certain chapters, entirely devoted to that subject have therefore been removed from the body of the book and printed as an appendix. This arrangement does not affect the sequence. (BMC)

His text then relegated this 'mystical matter' to an appendix, which directly marginalised the material in relation to what then becomes the main text but also subordinated it by decreasing the font size.

A comparison between Butler-Bowdon's list of de Worde's extracts and his own elisions reveals a degree of correlation. Precisely what de Worde found useful, Butler-Bowdon found extraneous. No doubt to some extent this reflects shifts in religious understanding. Butler-Bowdon expunges considerably more than de Worde printed. Almost all of his elisions are conversations between Kempe and Christ or accounts of her suffering in *imitatio Christi*, which perhaps struck the orthodox Catholic Butler-Bowdon as unnecessary.

In 1956, after the publication of the EETS edition, Oxford University Press republished the Butler-Bowdon modernisation, reproducing the manuscript's sequence in full and returning the so-called proem to the beginning of the volume. This modernised version has a higher degree of correspondence with the EETS edition, so that one can be used in conjunction with the other. The movement towards uniformity of presentation then begins to build a stable sense of what the book looks like, so that whether we read the modernised version or the scholarly edition, a more consistent picture emerges of what we mean by the *Book*.

Since 1936 and 1940, and these two first productions, *The Book of Margery Kempe* has appeared in many different contexts, and until very recently most of these have been aimed at a general, more popular market, and have been modernisations of various kinds. Louise Collis, for example, effectively re-wrote the book in her modernisation of the text published in the United States of America and England in 1964, intriguingly under different titles. For the English audience, Kempe the person was elided with the text itself, *The Apprentice Saint*, while Americans, rather less accurately, were presented with *Memoirs of a Medieval Woman: The Life and Times of Margery Kempe*. A remark early on in Collis' book, where she acknowledges that the picture of the life and times is remarkably selective, illustrates the strategy that Collis adopted. Where the text has absences or gaps, Collis interprets and extemporises. 'As she [Kempe] did not find the state of childhood interesting,' she remarks, 'we are told nothing of her life before marriage.'[11] Fundamentally, Collis seeks to make Kempe and her book comprehensible to a modern audience. She seeks to rid the text of its alien characteristics, to explain away awkwardnesses, to fill in the gaps of the text. Principally she does this through psychologising the characters, fleshing them out, providing them with motivations and reasons that are not transparent in the text. For example, a common experience of reading the *Book* is to wonder how

Kempe could confront religious authorities in the way described. How is it that, challenged by the Archbishop of York, Kempe continues to argue rather than obey his commands to leave his diocese? Collis addresses this issue directly: 'Either she took courage from the fact that he was fundamentally a just man who had been unable to find her guilty. Or else, recollecting the scene years afterwards as she dictated her book, she touched it up a bit in her own favour.'[12] The latter suggestion must have occurred to most people who read the text, at some point or another, but is not a suggestion that has been so confidently or simply stated as it is here. However, it is consistent with Collis' assumption of Kempe as apprentice saint and with more sophisticated accounts of the text's project or intent.

Nor is it Kempe alone who is rendered plausible to a modern audience, more interested in character, psychological consistency, and integrity than spiritual guidance. The archbishop's own behaviour to Kempe is similarly editorialised. We need wonder no longer why he put up with Kempe: 'He was rather coming round to Margery. There was something robust and honest about her that appealed to him.'[13] Referring to Kempe as Margery throughout, explaining why she acts in certain ways, providing stage directions and character descriptions, Collis renders the events and people of the text familiar and knowable. While Kempe herself is still awkward, 'insufferable,' 'uninhibited,' and gets on people's nerves,[14] this version of her text explains why. Collis' book then illustrates the interpretive aspects of translation.

She also tries to make the text less foreign for the modern reader in other ways. Like Butler-Bowdon, she recognised the different tastes of a modern audience and reduced the length and number of descriptions of Kempe's visions, and her lengthy conversations with Christ. In place of these, Collis inserts accounts of a more general kind relevant to the events and scenes to which Kempe refers. Often Collis leaves the matter of the *Book* itself for a foray into descriptions of medieval pilgrimages, travel, food, and customs. She thus contextualises the scenes that Kempe describes and in some ways provides the detail of the context with which the *Book* itself is not concerned; as the scribe explains in Book 2: 'Yf þe namys of þe placys be not ryth wretyn, late no man merueylyn, for sche stodyid mor a-bowte contemplacyon þan þe namys of þe placys, and he þat wrot hem had neuyr seyn hem, & þerfor haue hym excusyd' (233:8–12). ('If the names of places are not accurately recorded let no one be surprised, for she cared more about contemplation than place-names, and he who wrote them down had never seen them, so excuse him.')The illustrations provided also work to indicate how the text is part of and consistent with a medieval context that is represented by other texts and writings. In this way Collis authenticates Kempe's book by indicating its connections to other known sources.

One particular episode in the *Book* has been treated so often and so differently both in critical commentaries and in anthologies and editions that it makes a nice touchstone of shifting values and interests reflected in the different formats and contexts of those productions. The story of the priest and the pear-tree, which is at the heart of chapter 52 of the manuscript and the EETS edition, is a very interesting one, and in the next chapter I analyse it in detail to provide an alternative reading of it to ones that have gone before. At this point, however, I use it as a point of comparisons in editions, anthologies, and modernisations.

Put briefly, the story involves a description of a priest who is confronted by the vision of a bear who grabs and gobbles the beautiful flowers of a pear-tree and then reproduces them after they have been through his digestive system. Or, as it is described with the characteristic vividness of Kempe's language, and the directness of Chaucer himself: 'Gredily þis greuows best ete & deuowryd þo fayr flowerys. &, whan he had etyn hem, turnyng hys tayl-ende in þe prestys presens, voydyd hem owt ageyn at þe hymyer [hyndyr] party' (126:33–127:20.) ('Greedily, this dreadful bear ate and devoured the fair flowers and, when he had eaten them, turning his tail end in the priest's presence, voided them out again from his rear end.') As the anecdote develops, Kempe goes on to make connections between priest and bear. It is one of those breath-taking situations that makes one wonder about the bravery or foolhardiness of Kempe's behaviour. She has been accused of anti-clericalism and dares to re-tell this tale that on the surface seems to prove the case against her. Part of the shock of the scene to a modern audience is precisely the rudeness of it, and there is a tendency to become so hooked at the level of imagery, of the greedy and defecating bear, that the message is submerged. This Collis attempts to avoid through a writing-down of the story, a bowdlerisation that flattens out the story and removes some of its impact. Collis' version appears in chapter 36, with the title focussed on the hierarchical centre of the story, 'The Archbishop of York at Cawood.' Inspired to test out the accusation, because as Collis tells us the archbishop was 'rather coming round' to Kempe, he then hears a modified version. Here the bear is naughty rather than subversive, he 'gobbled all the blossom and then, turning round, was very dirty.'[15] In this account the archbishop finds the story valuable, as does the cleric who accused her in the first place, and we are again provided with an explanation as to his motivation that the original does not give us: 'At this unexpected reaction, the cleric hastened to say that he thought so too and sat down in some confusion.'[16]

In this context the difficulties the story presents for a modern audience, its abrasiveness, are sanded away, as a part of Collis' normalising process.

Collis' text then goes further than Butler-Bowdon's in re-writing the *Book* with some sense of a modern reader in mind. While the latter did remove sections of the text that he assumed would be of lesser interest to the audience, by and large his translations are literal and faithful to the tone of the original, whereas Collis' is a more impressionistic piece. In Collis we have a Kempe quaintly sanitised in some ways, censored and repackaged for a general reader.

Windeatt's translation of 1985 returns to the Butler-Bowdon style of faithfulness to the text. His modernisation keeps uniformity with the structure of the EETS text and is therefore suitable as an accessible companion to that volume for a student. As a paperback, the book is also accessible in terms of cost and effectively brought *The Book of Margery Kempe* to its widest audience. Its brief but informative notes provide contextual and historical information about people and places, dates and events, and its select bibliography provides further reading for the student or interested general reader. Given that Windeatt is also a Cambridge academic in English, this text also marks a moment in the history of Kempe studies where the promulgation of the text is linked with tertiary institutions, literature in particular, and aimed at undergraduates, rather than with religious communities or intent, and a non-specialised editor and audience. At one level, the audience of the text is expanded, as it is now not read or assumed to be interesting purely for its religious content. With a broadening of the education sector and a movement away from an understanding that medieval literature could only be approached in the original language, the audience among students for a text like *The Book of Margery Kempe* was considerably expanded. A translated text might be of interest to historians, literature students, or women's studies students. Yet at the same time, the fact that it could be approached from an academic angle, as a text in a curriculum, affords it a different kind of status, and, contradictorily, while expanding the audience in terms of size or numbers of readers, might well also involve a movement away from a general readership to a more specialized or élite audience. For now the *Book* is a Penguin Classic and is a volume on the shelves of the educated reader. The picture on the front cover of the Penguin edition exemplifies some of the contradictions in this production of *The Book of Margery Kempe*. The *Book*, which has itself become an object of study, in a portable, readable, accessible form, shows a figure that, to those who have not yet read the *Book*, could be taken for Kempe herself. She sits in a domestic location, on a stool, by a fire, stirring a pot, illustrating the homely and familiar objects that are so much a part of Kempe's book. Unlike Kempe, though, this medieval woman can clearly read, as while attending to her domestic duties, she glances at the book resting on her knee. In this sense the figure is, like Collis' Kempe, rather more like the modern reader than Kempe herself. Here is a female figure securely located in a domestic context but nevertheless with a secondary occupation. While it is debatable whether it is appropriate to label as 'illiterate' people like Kempe—who, while they probably could not read or write, nevertheless demonstrate a high level of what could be called cultural literacy, an understanding of texts and arguments and an ability to speak cogently about them—this picture is highly appropriate to a series like Penguin Classics, which attempts to develop, define, and promote traditions of literature to a wide reading public. The book as an artefact is both a crucial implement in the transference of cultures through time and down through generations of readers and a commodity in the market. In this context Kempe's appearance as a Penguin Classic is part of a move towards a different kind of canonisation from the one that she might originally have intended.

Two other translations of *The Book of Margery Kempe* in the last decade signal other kinds of values that are quintessentially modern rather than medieval. Catalogued in terms of subject matter, firstly as biography, secondly as women's studies, thirdly as Christian pilgrims and pilgrimages, and fourthly as mysticism, Tony D. Triggs' 'new' translation was published in 1995 by Triumph Books as a Triumph Classic.[17] The *Book* here sustains its identity crisis in the ambiguity over genre—whether it is biography or autobiography—as the full title of the text is *The Autobiography of the Madwoman of God: The Book of Margery Kempe*. In this encounter with the text, the reader is both assured of Kempe's orthodoxy and promised eccentrism and the exotic. The backcover blurb stresses Kempe's idiosyncracies and offers 'intriguing revelations,' 'an amazing story,' and 'spell-binding speeches,' that will 'fascinate modern readers.'

Retaining the structure of the manuscript, Butler-Bowdon's English edition and the EETS text, with one exception, and separating the text into clearly distinguishable chapters, Triggs' book also shares some characteristics with the Collis version. Where the latter reorganised the material into thematically re-structured chapters with illustrative titles, Triggs' text provides descriptive or impressionistic running headers that in some ways mimic the newspaper headlines and subheadlines that were such a feature of the early newspaper reviews. So we have 'Turned out of the Hostel,' 'From Bristol to Santiago and Back,' and 'Margery's Son—A Changed Man.'[18] The one exception to the structure is that Triggs moves the section that occurs in the manuscript at the end of chapter 18 to put it at the end of chapter 19, following suggestions made in notes to both the EETS and Windeatt editions.[19]

The most significant change that Triggs makes, however, and it is one shared by a second translation three years later, is in turning *The Book of Margery Kempe* into a first-person narrative. The result of this is a different kind of familiarity to that created by Collis' text, to which Triggs refers. The simple replacement of 'I' for 'she,' 'Margery' for 'this creatur,' provides a feeling of immediacy that the original text does not have. This translation is much more memoir and autobiography than treatise: 'This translation from the Middle English makes a confident choice in favour of allowing Margery to speak for herself throughout; we hear her account in the first person, just as her scribes must have heard it themselves.'[20] For Triggs this is part of an attempt to reproduce the authenticity of the text, as he particularly takes to task Collis' editorialising.

> [T]he locutions which Margery attributes to God show little sign of priestly editing. Some are sublime but most are banal—so much so that Louise Collis, in her book about Margery Kempe entitled *The Apprentice Saint* (Michael Joseph, 1964) mocks their banality by rounding off quotations with words like 'God remarked'. This translation attempts to preserve the original in all its range and variety, including its revealing flaws.[21]

Triggs' text offers a sense of interiority and psychological plausibility in a different way to Collis. Where Collis offers explicit editorial interpretations, Triggs offers insight into the mind of Kempe through the first-person pronoun, sugggesting a knowable and trustworthy narrator, with whom the reader can be in direct contact. Turning again to chapter 52 we can find examples of the differences that these editorial changes make to the meanings of the text. The clerk who has accused Kempe of anti-clerical tales, who agrees with the archbishop in Collis' version as an act of calculated self-protection, admits in the original that "'þis tale smytyth me to þe hert'" (127:37). There Kempe goes on to give another story about a priest who refused to give up admonishing the people for corrupt behaviour.

> He seyth many tymes in þe pulpit, 'ʒyf any man be euyl plesyd wyth my prechyng, not hym wel, for he is gylty.' And ryth so, ser,' seyd sche to þe clerk, 'far ye be me, God forʒeue it ʒow.' (128:4–7)

Kempe's alignment here is with the good priest, and the sense of herself as vehicle for God is evident not only in what the text says but how it is expressed. Just as the people are treated by the priest, so is he treated by her, where the sense of Kempe's agency or activity in this process is mitigated with the preposition 'by.' In Triggs' account we see a much more active and determined Kempe working on others: "'I'm causing you just the same discomfort," I said to the scholar. "May God forgive you.'"[22]

John Skinner's translation in 1998 adopts the same practice of turning the *Book* into a first-person narrative, and, produced by an ex-Jesuit and journalist, it carries different sets of expectations and values. Skinner nevertheless connects himself with previous strands of writing about Kempe that focussed on the quality and significance of writing in the English language. In his introduction we can see the same evolutionary sense of language that we saw in O'Connell's description of a development reaching apotheosis in Thomas More.[23] Skinner replaces one literary hero with another.

> It was not simply that Margery Kempe, like almost every woman of her day, was uneducated; the English language itself was still a spoken language. Its spelling was uncertain, its grammar and syntax still rudimentary; the very soil it sought to grow in was as yet undrained and, above all, still waiting to enjoy to the full the richly dunged matrix of its complex linguistic past. It would be another two centuries before the advent of printing and the rush of learning, when suddenly William Shakespeare would celebrate the fullness of that harvest crying out to be reaped.[24]

While there may be differences of opinion about when the peak was actually achieved and who best represents the finest flowers of Englishness, there is a consistency about this sense of progressive evolutionism. So Kempe is also included in Basil Cottle's *The Triumph of English 1350–1400*,[25] which, circumscribed by the dates, only extends to the first few pages of the manuscript.

Skinner's text is also aimed at pleasing the modern reader, as a paperback text to some extent must address its financial market, so he writes of his aims. In 'achieving a fresh version from the Middle English, it seems more important to offer today's readers a lively account by loosening the language, rather then adhering to the literal tautness of the Mount Grace version.'[26] Like Triggs, he follows the structure of the Salthouse manuscript in replicating the chapter divisions, with two exceptions. The first occurs where he, like Triggs, moves a section from chapter 18 to chapter 19, although this amendment is not acknowledged in his text. A second amendment he does reference, however, when his text moves chapter 21, so that it follows chapter 16 to give a clearer sense of chronology to Kempe's 'unfolding story.'[27]

Skinner's text is clearly a modernisation, while nevertheless cueing readers with images associated with the medieval period. The front and backcovers of his book use as a border a detail from *The Canterbury Tales* in the Huntington Library's collection. His footnotes refer to marginal annotations on the Salthouse manuscript and offer historical information about events and people as well as theological corrections to the errant Kempe's understanding.[28] Skinner's intention to make the *Book* as lively as he can for a modern audience can also be demonstrated through a small but amusing incident from the story of the priest and the pear-tree. Where Collis sanitises, and both Triggs and Skinner emphasise the sense of Kempe's agency through the first-person narrative,[29] Skinner goes further to bring the picture to the senses of the modern audience. Confronted with the rudeness of the 'greouws best,' the 'grete and boistows' bear (126:33 & 31), originally we were presented with the following predicament: 'Þe preste, hauyng gret abhominacyon of þat lothly syght, concey[ed] gret heuynes for dowte what it myth mene' (127:2–4). Skinner graphically redraws the scene to bring out the assault on the priest by adding one more sensory dimension to the story: 'The priest was revolted by this disgusting sight and the smell; at the same time he was disturbed, wanting to know what it meant.'[30]

Between these two translations, Lynn Staley's edition of *The Book of Margery Kempe* for the Middle English Texts Series and the Consortium for the Teaching of the Middle Ages (TEAMS) introduced a new kind of hybrid to the field of Kempe studies. The purposes of this series are clear: to produce in an accessible format, both in terms of cost and understanding, medieval texts which are otherwise difficult to access. In terms of Middle English editions, this was certainly true of *The Book of Margery Kempe* prior to the TEAMS text. While the EETS edition is undoubtedly the version with the most information, best notes, most extensive glossary and is most durable because of its hardback format; all of these features render it expensive and prohibitive for most undergraduate study. The TEAMS text puts *The Book of Margery Kempe* right into the classroom. It is now easier to teach the *Book* alongside other texts in Middle English without resorting to a translation, so that it can be treated with some kind of parity with other medieval texts. For the first time we had an affordable volume that is not a modernisation.

However, the TEAMS text is a hybrid that encapsulates a sense of anxiety about medieval literature and how it is taught. While the format is clear and elegant, it straddles a sense of Middle and modern English. While the series modernises the uses of u/v and j/i, Staley's *Book* also replaces thorns and yoghs so that the text has a curious half Middle English, half modern English look to it. There seem to be contradictions between the aims of accessibility and authenticity here. In that context, too, the glossary provided simply does not approach the usefulness of that supplied by the EETS edition, and the compromise between a text that can be used for study and one that does not intimidate a student through complex linguistic paraphernalia does not seem a particularly happy one. Bringing *The Book of Margery Kempe* into the classroom here has involved a kind of re-dressing that raises significant questions about what it is we are trying to do when we teach medieval literature. Further useful contributions to the dissemination of the *Book* in accessible formats have been Lynn Staley's modernised version for Norton and Barry Windeatt's annotated Middle English text.[31]

Aside from treatments of the whole text, *The Book of Margery Kempe* has been revisited and undergone new kinds of plunderings. Kempe never refers to herself as a mystic[32] and is not so identified in the sixteenth-century texts, and it was in the 1910 re-publication of Pepwell's collection that she achieved this position. It was the twentieth century that conferred the status of mystic upon Kempe. Edmund G. Gardner's text was entitled *The Cell of Self-Knowledge: Seven Early English Mystical Treatises*.[33] Since then Kempe's position has been cemented in relation to mysticism, and, since the publication of the full text, extracts from the text have been included in anthologies of mystical writing from works like Eric Colledge's *The Medieval Mystics of England* in 1961 to Barry Windeatt's *English Mystics of the Middle Ages* in 1994.[34] Aside from this specific positioning of Kempe as mystic, it is as a representative of religious experience that she often finds herself exhibited in twentieth-century anthologies, whether categorised under 'religious prose' or as exemplifying 'the medieval *summum bonum*, the vision of God.'[35]

With the development, and then expansion, of English as a discipline, the guises in which Kempe appears change significantly. No longer is Kempe's interest limited to those specialising in medieval literature but is extended to those studying literature generally or women in literature. Perhaps one of the most significant milestones in the dissemination of *The Book of Margery Kempe* occurred in 1979, when the Norton Anthology, first published in 1962, included extracts from the *Book*. Here, indeed, there is an interesting reversal in the usual hierarchy of positions enjoyed by Kempe and Julian of Norwich, as the latter only joined the Norton Anthology in the sixth edition in 1993. Norton's status as undergraduate study text exposes Kempe to a far wider audience than she has been exposed to before, and it is revealing that while the sixth edition already contains extracts from six chapters, the seventh edition, published in 1999, includes an extra one.[36]

As might be expected of an anthology that intends to demonstrate the diversity and range of writing by women in English and the longevity of women's literary history, both Julian of Norwich and Margery Kempe appear in Norton's sister volume, *Literature by Women: The Traditions in English*, in the first edition of

1985 and the second edition of 1996, although there is less of Kempe in *Literature by Women* than there is in *The Norton Anthology of English Literature*, again demonstrating the perceived significance of Kempe in the development of specifically English literature and language. The kind of material also varies between the two Norton texts. *Literature by Women* includes the Butler-Bowdon translation of chapters 3, 4 and 11, all of which are concerned with the physical, sexual body of Margery Kempe and her struggles with sexual issues. Chapter 3, for example, concerns Kempe hearing sweet melodies that make her want to separate from her husband, her repentance of her previous life, and her pleas for chastity, which others interpret as hypocrisy. Chapter 4 involves her temptation to adultery and her embarrassing but salutary rejection, and chapter 11 is the often-anthologised chapter concerning Kempe's successful negotiations with her husband to release her from her conjugal duties: 'It befell on a Friday on Midsummer Eve in right hot weather....'[37]

The Norton Anthology of English Literature also produces extracts in modern English although these are newly done from the EETS text. These extracts cover a broader range of material, from accounts of Kempe's illness, Christ's interventions, the meeting with Julian of Norwich, the pilgrimage to Jerusalem, and her examination by senior clergy.[38] This Norton also includes chapter 52, which begins with Kempe's interview by the Archbishop of York but omits the story of the priest and the pear-tree, as does Derek Pearsall's 1999 *From Chaucer to Spenser*.[39] It is significant that both of these provide brief summaries of the tale rather than the tale itself, while Windeatt's volume, *English Mysticism of the Middle Ages*, includes the tale in full, indicating the different contexts of the books, Norton's and Pearsall's being predominantly secular, Windeatt's predominantly religious. It is in the latter that the tale makes most sense and has most resonance.

The Book of Margery Kempe has also recently increased its number of appearances in collections or contexts focussed specifically on women or gender, regardless of the historical or religious aspects of her specific context. So Jane Robinson's aim is to put alongside histories of men's travel, a collection of '*first-hand* travel accounts *in book form*' by women, and her book includes summaries of Kempe's pilgrimages.[40] Quite literally, Kempe here marches alongside other fellow travellers, the links between whom are provided by the aims of the editor. In this quite different situational context Kempe is tagged as a pioneer, distant from the figure whose anxieties about the opinions of her contemporaries is so marked in the whole *Book*. Kempe is also re-written in this context to include a different sense of the wayward from the one that emerges from her book. Wayward here includes a sense of resistance to the strictures imposed by society on women's physical movement, so that Kempe's story becomes part of the history of women's struggles against such limitations.

In a similar way Kempe is recuperated for a history of the metaphysical and psychological travels of women and the history of the recording of those travels through being included in Mary Grimley Mason's and Carol Hurd Green's *Journeys: Autobiographical Writings by Women*.[41] While it is evident that *The Book of Margery Kempe* is more treatise than reflective self-analysis, here it becomes part of the history of women's records of their own lives, where gender and writing provide the basis for the situational context. The development of a specifically female audience, aware of and interested in issues of gender and sexuality, provides criteria for collections that discriminate primarily on gender grounds rather than specific content.

This has been particularly noticeable in the last twenty years in popular fiction that is woman centred, and Margery Kempe has appeared here too. Sheri S. Tepper's *Beauty*, for example, is part of the modern fantasy genre, focussing on women characters. Margery Kempe appears in this context to add historical ballast in the attempt to develop an atmosphere that is perceptibly different from twentieth-century daily life. The text is divided into short, titled sections that give the novel a sense of originating in history and fact rather than fiction. Kempe's appearance is in a section headed 'Corpus Christi Day,' specified as 1417 in the previous section.

> A procession in honor of the Blessed Sacrament came winding through the streets today. Outside the hostel a crazy woman had a fit when she saw it and had to be dragged away, screaming and yelling. I am told her name is Margery Kempe. In the twentieth century they would probably have put the poor thing on tranquilizers and put her to bed, but at this time she is quite notorious. She goes on incessant pilgrimages, falling continually into these hysterical fits, and she has evidently been doing so for years…there is no doubt that she is seriously disturbed….[42]

Tepper's formulation has more in common with Oliver Sacks' analysis of Hildegard of Bingen than with medieval attitudes to either woman. Sacks unproblematically describes Hildegard's visions as 'indisputably migrainous,' thus rendering these events comprehensible to a modern, scientific world.[43] Kempe's behaviour is seen as clinically treatable in a way that ignores the contexts of the experience. Yet *Beauty* is ambivalent about the provenance of these phenomena and refuses to write out the existence of the divine, preferring instead the possibility that Kempe's experiences legitimate her and instantiate her as female prophet: '*Three days later:* Still no wind. The pilgrims are beginning to regret their hostility. I heard one say today there would be no wind until Margery Kempe returned, that no matter what the pilgrims may think, God is with her.'[44] Kempe mediates differences between contemporary and earlier life, yet for both she exemplifies the difficulties of women's experience. In this perhaps more than anything else lies her value for contemporary popular fiction directed at female audiences. Tepper, like Marion Bradley in *The Mists of Avalon*,[45] constructs history and mythology that are women centred. Popular fiction of this kind can be seen to be experimenting with the kind of 'feminine divine' proposed by Luce Irigaray, where the project is to construct a metaphysics that is as inspired by understandings of femininity, or woman centredness, as the Christian religion has been said to be by masculinity.[46] While *The Book of Margery Kempe* articulates the material and ideological struggles of Kempe for religious self-expression, in something like *Beauty* Kempe becomes part of an exploration of the possibilities of Woman that renders her a metaphor and, in that sense, de-materialises her.

Perhaps the most elaborate use of Kempe, the most flamboyant dress in which she appears, is in Robert Glück's novel of homosexual love, *Margery Kempe*.[47] Its narrative structure consists of re-telling the story of Margery Kempe in parallel with the narrator's account of his passion for a younger lover. The central conceit is a comparison of Kempe's passion for Jesus with the narrator's passion for his lover. Tracking between the fifteenth and twentieth centuries, the novel makes comparisons between the humility and self-abnegation of the religious experience and the obsessions of mortal lovers. For readers of this paperback, a specifically targeted audience of gay readers, Kempe becomes part of the exploration of homosexual desire, and she is dressed accordingly. Glück's use of Collis' *Memoirs of a Medieval Woman* is evident in the construction of Kempe as a knowable, identifiable character. While for Collis, Triggs, Skinner, and Glück, Kempe is 'Margery,' Glück exemplifies this sense of familiarity through annihilating the gap between narrator, 'Bob,' and Kempe: 'As Margery, I wake up and enter the dark street hoping to catch a glimpse of Jesus and trying to avoid him.'[48]

Painfully embodied in Glück's novel, Kempe encapsulates a modern obsession with desire, individuality, and personality. In Howard Nemerov's piece, 'A Poem of Margery Kempe,' a similar concentration on self-examination is at work, in distinct contrast to the *Book*'s creature. While Nemerov's poem is 'of' or about Kempe, it is written as if from her point of view. The opening lines set the tone:

I creature being now mad
They locked me in my room.[49]

In the thirty-two short lines of the poem, the self-consciousness of Kempe is emphasised through eleven uses of the pronoun 'I,' and twelve occurrences of 'me' or 'my.'[50]

If all of these examples indicate the changes made to *The Book of Margery Kempe* for modern purposes and audiences, one other example illustrates the pitfalls of not modifying a text with the audience in mind. King's Lynn, as one might expect, has made much of its famous citizen, including references to her in its pamphlets on St Margaret's Church and its tourist leaflets, and from time to time, Kempe appears in local summer festivals. In July 1973 local musicians the Throseby Consort and the Sturdy Beggars combined with soloists to perform 'Margery Kempe at St Margaret's,' providing, through words and song, 'Glimpses of life in Bishop's Lynn in the early 1400s through the eyes of the devout but unstoppable Margery Kempe.'[51] While the reaction to this public event is not on record, the reaction to another local event for local people is. Designed to tour Yorkshire and East Anglia after its world premiere on Tuesday, May 9, 1978, Roger Howard's work, *The Play of Margery Kempe* was performed in The Fermoy Center, King's Street, King's Lynn. A short play, the text of the performance features a pilgrim in cowl on its cover and maintains its faith with the Salthouse manuscript and the EETS edition through including the character of Margery Kempe, who talks about herself in the third person. In short vignettes, the text traverses Kempe's life from early illness, through her various physical temptations to the collapse of the beam in St Margaret's Church and the Guildhall fire, to her prayers at the end of the second book. At the conclusion of the script, the text calls for a pause before the house lights go up and, rather optimistically as it turned out, for the playing of a 'jolly piece for the Curtain Calls.' According to the review in the *Eastern Daily Press* the next day, overall the play 'left its audience more than a little puzzled.' Another review of the same performance records that far from rapt applause and multiple curtain calls at this account of one of Lynn's most famous daughters what occurred was 'audience silence at the end of the 70-minute performance.'[52] While the reviewer went on to lament local ignorance of its history, it is also at least as plausible that a late 1970s audience simply could not relate to the episodic style of the play and the ambiguous sense of self that a figure who consistently refers to herself in the third person displays. Here we see, in the audience reaction, the perils of not adapting a text for a modern audience.

Every time Kempe appears in a modern text she is re-written, most conspicuously in these most recent texts, demonstrating modern concerns with personality, psychological plausibility, and individualism. Indeed, failure to do so endangers the success of the text and threatens to consign it to oblivion as the unfortunate Howard play testifies. If Kempe is present in these texts then it is through an act of ventriloquism, where she provides a body, dressed in varying fashions, whose lips move to other people's words. There are many books of Margery Kempe, many different contexts in which she occurs, many ways in which her name is invoked, and each of these tells us at least as much about the contexts in which they are re-produced as it does about the original context in the fifteenth century. Kempe is made and re-made, as is her *Book*. If the transition from medieval spiritual guide, from manuscript to paperback textbook are significant shifts in situational contexts, then nowhere is this more pronounced than in the shift from apprentice saint to gay icon.

Notes

1. Sue Ellen Holbrook, '"About Her": Margery Kempe's Book of Feeling and Working,' eds. James M. Dean and Christian K. Zacher, *The Idea of Medieval Literature: New Essays on Chaucer and Medieval Culture in Honor of Donald R. Howard* (Newark: University of Delaware Press, 1992).

2. Raymond Williams, *Problems in Materialism and Culture* (London: Verso, 1980), pp. 46 & 44.

3. Paul Eggert, ed., *Editing in Australia* (Canberra: Australian Defence Force Academy, 1990), p. 27. This collection of papers from the conference on editing includes work by Hans Walter Gabler and Peter L. Shillingsburg, and it is the latter's work that Eggert is here summarising. Shillingsburg himself writes of the way 'that the linguistic text generates only a part of the meaning of a book; its production, its price, its cover, its margin, its type font all carry meaning that can be documented. In short, the physical book, of which the linguistic text is but a part, is important not because we have become accustomed to it, and not merely because it is a part of history, but because its form and historical entry into the culture determined the cultural acceptance it received,' Peter L. Shillingsburg, 'An Inquiry into the Social Status of Texts and Modes of Textual Criticism,' *Studies in Bibliography*, 42, 1989, p. 64.

4. D. F. McKenzie, *Bibliography and the Sociology of Texts*, The Panizzi Lectures (London: The British Library, 1985), pp. 6–7.

5. Sue Ellen Holbrook, 'Margery Kempe and Wynkyn de Worde,' *The Medieval Mystical Tradition*, ed. Marion Glasscoe (Cambridge: D. S. Brewer, 1987); Karma Lochrie, *Margery Kempe and Translations of the Flesh* (Philadelphia: University of Pennsylvania Press, 1991), chapter 6.

6. Holbrook, ibid., pp. 40 and 42.

7. Lochrie, op. cit., p. 227.

8. Holbrook, '"About Her,"' p. 35.

9. John M. Ganim, 'The Myth of Medieval Romance,' *Medievalism and the Modern Temper*, eds. R. Howard Bloch and Stephen G. Nichols (Baltimore: The Johns Hopkins University Press, 1996), p. 155.

10. W. Butler-Bowdon, *The Book of Margery Kempe 1436: A Modern Version* (London: Jonathan Cape, 1936), p. 16.

11. Louise Collis, *The Apprentice Saint* (London: Michael Joseph, 1964), *Memoirs of a Medieval Woman: The Life and Times of Margery Kempe* (New York: Harper & Row, 1964), p. 9.

12. Ibid., p. 204.

13. Ibid., p. 205.

14. Ibid., pp. 204, 119 and 217.

15. Ibid., p. 205.

16. Ibid., p. 206.

17. Tony D. Triggs, *The Autobiography of the Madwoman of God: 'The Book of Margery Kempe'* (Ligouri, Missouri: Triumph Books, 1995).

18. These are the headings for Book 1, chapters 31 (p. 77), 45 (p. 101), & Book 2, chapter 2 (p. 189), respectively.

19. Of all the changes made to the text by various editions, this one does seem to make the most sense in terms of the coherence of the content. See Tony D. Triggs, p. 12.

20. Ibid.

21. Ibid.

22. Tony D. Triggs, p.115.

23. See the discussion in the previous chapter.

24. John Skinner, *The Book of Margery Kempe* (New York: Image Books, Doubleday; 1998), p. 4.

25. Basil Cottle, *The Triumph of English 1350–1400* (London: Blandford Press, 1969).

26. Ibid.

27. Ibid., p. 66.

28. See, for example, Skinner's observation in a footnote to chapter 78 on Kempe's reference to taking mass: 'Margery's imagination is racing: there is no mass on Good Friday, merely distribution of communion,' p. 259. The EETS text and Butler-Bowdon translation reproduce the Salthouse manuscript's reference here to 'Messe-tyme,' rather than 'Messe.' Triggs has 'mass', p. 160.

29. In response to the clerk's 'confusion' at the end of the tale, Skinner has Kempe's response: 'And I am reminded of you, sir, how you have treated me. May God forgive you for it,' p. 184. This does not have the voluntaristic strength that we see in Triggs' version, and the second clause conveys the sense of Kempe as operated on rather than operating, but the presence of the first-person pronoun neverthess conveys the impression of will and determination not in the original version.

30. John Skinner, p. 183.

31. *The Book of Margery Kempe*, translated and edited, Lynn Staley (New York: W.W. Norton and Co., 2001) is an edition with contexts and criticism; *The Book of Margery Kempe*, ed. Barry Windeatt (Essex: Longman, 2000).

32. See Sue Ellen Holbrook, '"About Her,"' p. 267.

33. *The Cell of Self-Knowledge: Seven Early English Mystical Treatises printed by Henry Pepwell in 1521*, edited and with an introduction and notes by Edmund G. Gardner (New York: Cooper Square Publishing Inc., 1910).

34. *The Medieval Mystics of England*, edited with an introduction by Eric Colledge (New York; Charles Scribner's Sons, 1961); Barry Windeatt, *English Mystics of the Middle Ages* (Cambridge: Cambridge University Press, 1994).

35. See *The Oxford Book of Medieval Prose*, ed. Douglas Gray (Oxford: Oxford University Press, 1988), where the extracts are in Middle English; and *The Portable Medieval Reader*, eds. James Bruce Ross and Mary Martin McLaughlin (Harmondsworth: Penguin, 1977), p. 27, where the extracts are modernised, respectively.

36. I am grateful to Christina Grenawalt from W. W. Norton & Co. for information about the inclusion of Chapter 76, in which Kempe cares for her husband.

37. *The Norton Anthology: Literature by Women: The Traditions in English*, eds. Sandra M. Gilbert and Susan Gubar (New York: W. W. Norton & Co., 1996), p. 23.

38. The extracts are from chapters 1, 2, 11, 18, 28, and 52.

39. *From Chaucer to Spenser*, ed. Derek Pearsall (Oxford: Blackwell, 1999).

40. Jane Robinson, *Wayward Women: A Guide to Women Travellers* (Oxford: Oxford University Press, 1991), p. x.

41. Mary Grimley Mason & Carol Hurd Green, eds., *Journeys: Autobiographical Writings by Women* (Boston, Massachusetts: G. K. Hall & Co., 1979).

42. Sheri S. Tepper, *Beauty* (London: Grafton, 1993), pp. 337–8. I am grateful to Anne Cranny-Francis for this reference.

43. Oliver Sacks, *The Man Who Mistook His Wife for a Hat* (London: Picador, 1985), p. 160.

44. Ibid., p. 338.

45. Marion Bradley, *The Mists of Avalon* (London: Sphere Books Ltd., 1982).

46. Luce Irigaray, *Divine Women* (Sydney: Local Consumption, 1986). Liz Gross provides a useful analysis of this paper, *Irigaray and the Divine* (Sydney: Local Consumption, 1986).

47. Robert Glück, *Margery Kempe* (London: High Risk Books/Serpent's Tail, 1994).

48. Ibid, p. 87.

49. Howard Nemerov, 'A Poem of Margery Kempe,' *The Collected Poems of Howard Nemerov* (Chicago: Chicago University Press, 1977).

50. This count excludes the refrain 'Alas! that ever I did sin,/It is full merry in heaven,' which occurs after each of the four stanzas.

51. Publicity material produced by sponsors Network SouthEast.

52. This material is held in the Lynn Museum and Lynn Townhouse Museum collections. The first review is by 'G. W.,' 10 May 1978 in the *Eastern Daily Press*, while the clipping of the second review by Richard Parr does not indicate its provenance. This latter is also annotated 12–6–78, when it must mean 12–5–78, given that it is a review of the premiere performance too.

Chapter 7

The One About the Bear:
A Cultural Materialist Reading

This chapter provides a cultural materialist reading of a part of *The Book of Margery Kempe*, a part which has been a topic of discussion from the earliest criticism to the most recent. The passage from chapter 52 concerns an account of Kempe's encounter with church authorities and is annotated in the manuscript by one of its earliest readers. In the absence of any clear source, the story of the bear, the priest and the pear-tree also seems to be original to Kempe.[1] According to the varying purposes of particular editors, it has been sometimes omitted from selections of the *Book*, sometimes included in collections of extracts. It provides, then, a useful case for the exercise of a close reading that also considers the issues of production, reception, reproduction and dissemination. It stands as an example of the ways in whch *The Book of Margery Kempe* has been made and re-made in the period since its identification. Three quite different analyses of what, for the purposes of brevity, I shall call the bear story indicate changes within the criticism of the Kempe text over the seventy years since the discovery of the manuscript. Each treatment suggests not only historical shifts in criticism but also the concerns of the different interest groups that have focussed on Kempe.

Brought to York, probably in 1417, Kempe is accused by members of the archbishop's retinue of being a Lollard and a heretic. Once again confronted by Archbishop Henry Bowet, Kempe is challenged over the inappropriateness of her wearing white as a married woman and faces the ultimate challenge to the floating or unstable signifier, stasis: Bowet threatens to have her fettered to the spot as a 'fals heretyke' (124:19). Tested on and passing the articles of faith, Kempe refuses commands by Bowet that she leave York, and that she neither 'techyn ne chalengyn þe pepil' in his diocese (125:37–126: 1). Finally, when Kempe has countered all allegations concerning doctrinal heresy, a 'doctowr' (126:21) there present accuses her of telling anti-clerical tales. Because the story itself is fundamental to an understanding of the various interpretations that have been made of it, and particular features of it are central to my own approach, I quote the story in its entirety.

Than seyd a doctowr whech had examynd hir be-for-tyme, 'Syr, sche telde me þe werst talys of prestys þat euyr I herde.' Þe Bischop comawndyd hir to tellyn þat tale. 'Sir, wyth зowr reuerens, I spak but of o preste be þe maner of exampyl, þe whech as I haue lernyd went wil in a wode thorw þe sufferawns of God for þe profite of hys sowle tyl þe nygth cam up-on hym. He, destytute of hys herborwe, fond a fayr erber in þe whech he restyd þat nyght, hauyng a fayr pertre in þe myddys al floreschyd wyth flowerys & belschyd, and blomys ful delectabil to hys syght, wher cam a bere, gret & boistows, hogely to behelden, schakyng þe pertre & fellyng down þe flowerys. Gredily þis greuows best ete & deuowryd þo fayr flowerys. &, whan he had etyn hem, turnyng hys tayl-ende in þe prestys presens, voydyd hem owt ageyn at þe hymyr party. Þe preste, hauyng gret abhominacyon of þat lothly syght, conceyuyng gret heuynes for dowte what it myth mene, on þe next day he wandrid forth in hys wey al heuy & pensife, whom it fortunyd to metyn wyth a semly agydd man lych to a palmyr er a pilgrime, þe whiche enqwird of þe preste þe cawse of hys heuynes. The preste, rehersyng þe mater be-forn-wretyn, seyd he conceyuyd gret drede & heuynes whan he beheld þat lothly best defowlyn & deuowryn so fayr flowerys & blomys & aftirward so horrybely to deuoydyn hem be-for hym at hys tayl-ende, & he not vndirstondyng what þis myth mene. Than þe palmyr, schewyng hym-selfe þe massanger of God, þus aresond hym, "Preste, þu þi-self art þe pertre, sumdel florischyng & floweryng thorw þi Seruyse seyyng & þe Sacramentys ministryng, thow þu do vndeuowtly, for þu takyst ful lytyl heede how þu seyst þi Mateynes & þi Seruyse, so it be blaberyd to an ende. Þan gost þu to þi Messe wyth-owtyn deuocyon, & for þi synne hast þu ful lityl contricyon. Þu receyuyst þer þe frute of euyrlestyng lyfe, þe Sacrament of þe Awter, in ful febyl disposicyon. Sithyn al þe day aftyr þu myssespendist þi tyme, þu зeuist þe to byyng & sellyng, choppyng & chongyng, as it wer a man of þe werld. Þu sittyst at þe ale, зeuyng þe to glotonye & excesse, to lust of thy body, thorw letchery & vnclennesse. Þu brekyst þe comawndmentys of God throw sweryng, lying, detraccyon, & bakbytyng, & swech oþer synnes vsyng. Thus be thy mysgouernawns, lych on-to þe lothly ber, þu deuowryst & destroist þe flowerys & blomys of vertuows leuyng to thyn endles dampnacyon & many mannys hyndryng lesse þan þu haue grace of repentawns & amendyng." Þan þe Erchebisshop likyd wel þe tale & comendyd it, seyng it was a good tale. (126–7)

(Then a doctor who had examined her before said, 'Sir, she told me the worst tale about priests that I ever heard.' The bishop commanded her to tell that tale. 'Sir, with respect, I spoke but of one priest by manner of example, who, as I have learned, went astray in a wood, through the sufferance of God for the profit of his soul, until night came upon him. He, without anywhere to stay, found a fair arbour in which he rested that night, having a fair pear tree in the middle all adorned with flowers and embellished with blossoms delightful to the sight, where there came a bear, huge and violent, ugly to behold, shaking the pear tree and making the flowers fall. Greedily this dreadful beast ate and devoured those fair flowers. And, when he had eaten, turning his tail in the priest's presence, voided them out again from his rear end. The priest, having great disgust at that loathsome sight, experiencing great sorrow for uncertainty at what it might mean, on the next day he wandered forth on his way all depressed and pensive, when it fortuned him to meet a handsome, aged man like a palmer or a pilgrim, who enquired of the priest the reason for his sadness. The priest, rehearsing the matter written before, said he felt great fear and sorrow when he saw that loathsome beast defoul and devour such fair flowers and blossoms and afterwards so horribly to discharge them before him from his rear-end, and he not understanding what this might mean. Then the palmer showing himself to be the messenger of God, thus addressed him: 'Priest, you yourself are the pear tree, somewhat flourishing and blossoming through saying the services and administering the sacraments, though you do so without devotion, for you take very little heed how you say the matins and the service, so long as it is blabbered to an end. Then you go to Mass without devotion, and you have very little contrition for your sin. You receive there the fruit of everlasting life, the Sacrament of the Altar, in very feeble state of mind. Afterwards all the day after you misspend your time, you give yourself to buying and selling, chopping and changing [bartering] as if you were a man of the world. You sit drinking ale, giving yourself to gluttony and excess, to lust of the body, through lechery and impurity. You break the commandments of God through swearing, lying, detraction, and backbiting, and committing such other sins. Thus by your misconduct, like the loathsome bear, you devour and destroy the flowers and blossoms of virtuous living to your endless damnation and the detriment of many men unless you have grace to repent and amend.' Then the Archbishop liked the tale well and commended it, saying it was a good tale.)

As the marginal annotations indicate, this story was singled out by the first readers of the manuscript. While some of these annotations are difficult to read with the naked eye, there are clearly different inks in evidence on the manuscript. Of the four different ones, our story attracted the attention of two readers. As Meech puts it in his introduction to the EETS edition, the passage is annotated with '*narracio* in small brown letters in outer margin with *of þe preyst and þe pertre* in red beneath it' (126). There is considerable significance in these notations. First, and most obviously, the remarks indicate that at least two of the readers of the passage saw it as instructive and worth comment. *Narracio* here suggests that this is a story, a narrative, which is literally worth marking. The passage can be taken to be of greater note than other passages not so marked. *Narratio*, as a medieval Latin rhetorical term, also suggests that the passage is to be seen as *exemplum* or explanation, the significance of which I shall return to later.

Second, in terms of the material conditions under which the extant manuscript was produced, the passage provides one way of dating the annotations relative to each other. Clearly the red ink is the work of a later reader because it adds to and extends the remarks of the brown ink writer. The preposition 'of' indicates that the writer in red ink is relating to the words in brown ink that were previously already on the page by the time the red ink was added. The words on the page are not only significant in themselves for indicating the concerns of earlier readers, but the materiality of their existence, their relation to each other, also gives us information about the readers beyond the words on the page.[2] Meech deduces from an examination of the different annotations that the latest of the annotators was the writer in red ink, who, he also deduces, from the nature of the comments and their placement, was a 'monk at Mount Grace' (xxxvi).

Third, the second commentator, in the red ink, by the nature of the remarks, indicates those elements of the story that characterised its importance for him/her. So this passage is described as the story of the priest and the pear-tree, while the third element or character in the story that Kempe tells, the bear who commits the act that terrifies and perplexes the priest, is marginalised. This can be read as indicative of a different understanding of the story from modern readings. While contemporary readings focus on the recalcitrant and disruptive bear, the early readers focus on priest and pear-tree. It is indicative of historical shifts in interest that the bear, which symbolises the problems in the church, is omitted from the marginal comments that focus on the importance of the message rather than the specificities of its delivery.

In keeping with a focus on the spiritual significance of the story, one of the earliest interpreters of the book in the twentieth century also included comment on the priest and pear-tree story. A Benedictine of Stanbrook in 1938 shared the perceptions of his time that the *Book* threw 'a vivid light on everyday life in England five centuries ago.' In particular, the book illuminated 'religious faith and practice' and even more specifically 'in regard to the vital doctrine of the Holy Eucharist.'[3] To this Catholic reviewer these observations were interesting rather than particularly unusual. In other words, what Kempe had to say about religious practices was expected and orthodox from a Catholic perspective and provided material that the Benedictine might have expected to find in a history of fifteenth-century England. In this context he refers briefly to 'the moral tale of the pear-tree' as providing evidence of the perceived significance of the Mass, demonstrated through the negative example of the priest. For the Benedictine, the *Book* provides evidence for the 'reverence and devotion of fifteenth century England towards the Blessed Sacrament' through demonstrating its significance in Kempe's life.[4] The story of the priest is one example in the chain of proof.

More recently, a second, quite different approach to the bear story came from Karma Lochrie, in her challenging feminist book, *Margery Kempe and Translations of the Flesh*. Lochrie was concerned to reconsider and re-contextualise Kempe through activating a sense of her agency, attributing conscious intent to Kempe's actions, and refusing to see her as a victim of her times and male-dominated society. Yet Lochrie's book is not a crude recuperation of a woman in history for the modern feminist cause. As she put it, her purpose is not to 'rehabilitate Margery Kempe nor to claim her as a feminist' but to provide 'only one feminist approach to Margery Kempe which begins with the medieval body and ends with medieval scholarship today.'[5]

Lochrie sees the bear story, in her chapter 'Fissuring the Text: Laughter in the Midst of Writing and Speech,' as an example of the relationship between laughter and defilement, arguing that Kempe uses humour and laughter deliberately and consciously. 'She who laughs takes defilement on herself, making a spectacle of it, in order to disperse speech, authority, and models of holiness, where a culture's power is located.'[6] Arguing that 'laughter is subversive,' and that it 'threatens the very boundaries of social and institutional bodies,'[7] Lochrie sees the bear story as exemplifying Kempe's criticism of religious practices through humour. In this sense she rightly returns a dimension to the *Book* that has too often been missing from criticism.[8] While Lochrie takes Bakhtin's account of carnival and the grotesque body to task, refusing to adopt it because of its lack of gender awareness, her approach is nevertheless influenced by Bakhtinian models and by French feminist models of abjection and the body.[9] Transgression and subversion are terms that recur throughout the book and are part of her attempt to return to Kempe notions of agency and intentionality.

Three years later, Lynn Staley re-addressed the tale in her book *Margery Kempe's Dissenting Fictions*.[10] Making direct reference to Lochrie's account of the episode and Lochrie's discussion of Kempe as preacher, Staley's account varies in linking the episode back to Lollardy and the controversial issue of mass and transubstantiation. In so doing she provides a reading that is more historically grounded, locating the story in terms of contemporary debates and perspectives. The discussion occurs in the early stages of Staley's book and is part of her overall argument that Kempe is negotiating a path for herself through contemporary society. For her the tale occupies a position 'poised delicately somewhere between irony and criticism.'[11] In this context what follows is offered as an alternative feminist approach to Lochrie's and Staley's that is less antagonistic to either of them than suggestive of a difference in emphasis. The emphasis, however, is significant and part of an attempt to offer a feminist methodology that is materialist and avoids some of the reificatory and essentialising potential attached to notions of transgression and subversion.

In 1401 the statute *de haeretico comburendo* claimed its first victim; William Sawtre, parish priest of St Margaret's church in Lynn, was burnt at the stake.[12]

Although Sawtre had previously been accused of heresy and had repented, he returned to his heretical belief and 'teaching that "after consecration by the priest, the bread remaineth true material bread."'[13] Caroline Walker Bynum's study *Holy Feast and Holy Fast* identifies in the late medieval period a professionalisation of the clergy such that they mediated between God and the people to the extent of taking communion for them. Sawtre's anti-transubstantiation teaching needs to be put in the context of an increasingly protective attitude towards communion and the anxiety of those who 'feared that frequent reception [of communion] might lead to loss of reverence, to carelessness, even to profanation of the elements.'[14]

In this context Sawtre, as a priest, undermines the professional ethic from within and endangers the exalted role of the priest, threatening to diminish 'the gap between priest and people.'[15] Kempe, on the other hand, sought permission to take communion every Sunday and occasionally gained the right as a mark of her spiritual devotion.[16] Paradoxically, while Kempe and her 'masterless' position as independent, travelling laywoman can be seen historically as threatening the gap between priest and people, the story of 'þe priest and þe pertre' specifically concerns the sacred position of the ecclesiastical mediators through a negative exemplum.

On other occasions Kempe also evidences her concern with access to the sacraments of the Church and their crucial rôle in her spiritual life. In the first pages of the *Book* she makes quite clear her attachment to these offices and positions herself against those who would argue that the Christian soul can flourish without the benefice of the Church and clergy. So one of the ways in which the devil manifests his temptation is to try to lure Kempe away from the Church and then to bring her to despair. Kempe's account of this takes the form of exposing her error, describing her subsequent understanding and her return to the safety of the clergy.

> For sche was euyr lettyd be hyr enmy, þe Deuel, euyr-mor seyng to hyr whyl sche was in good heele hir nedyd no confessyon but don penawns be hir-self a-loone, & all schuld be forȝouyn, for God is mercyful j-now. And þerfor þis creatur oftyn-tymes dede greet penawns in fastyng bred & water & oþer dedys of alms wyth devowt preyers, saf sche wold not schewyn it in confessyon. And, whan sche was any tym seke or dysesyd, þe Deyl seyd in her mende þat sche schuld be dampnyd, for sche was not schreuyn of þat defawt. (7:1–11)

> (For she was always hindered by her enemy, the devil, who was always saying to her that while she was in good health she needed no confession, but could do penance by herself alone, and all would be forgiven, for God is merciful enough. And therefore this creature often did great penance in fasting upon bread and water, and other acts of charity with

devout prayers, except that she would not reveal it in confession. And, when she was at any time ill or troubled. the devil said in her mind that she would be damned because she had not confessed and been absolved of that fault)

The temptation that she comes to resist so successfully is to go it alone. Christ tells Kempe 'dowtyr, þis lyfe plesyth me mor þan weryng of þe haburion or of þe hayr or fastyng of bred & watyr, for, ȝyf þu seydest euery day a thousand Pater Noster, þu xuldist not plesyn me so wel as þu dost whan þu art in silens & sufferyst me to speke in thy sowle' (89:19–25), ('daughter, this life pleases me more than wearing a haburion [mail coat worn next to the skin] or a hair-shirt, or fasting upon bread and water, for, if you said a thousand Pater Nosters you should not please me as well as you do when you are silent and allow me to speak in your soul.'). The point seems to be not that she may neglect the offices of the Church but that it is the sincerity of her passion that validates her. The perfunctory going through the motions of the ordinances of the Church cannot compensate for true belief.

Similarly, when Kempe is brought before Richard Rothley, Abbot of Leicester, and is publicly tested on her knowledge of the Articles of the Faith, the one we hear in full is the 'blysful Sacrament of the Awter' (115:9).

> "Serys, I beleue in þe Sacrament of þe Awter on þis wyse, þat what man hath takyn þe ordyr of presthode, be he neuyr so vicyows a man in hys leuyng, ȝyf he sey dewly þo wordys ouyr þe bred þat owr Lord Ihesu Criste seyde whan he mad hys Mawnde a-mong hys disciplys þer he sat at þe soper, I be-leue þat it is hys very flesch & hys blood & no material bred ne neuyr may be vnseyd be it onys seyd." (115:10–18)

> ("Sirs, I believe in the Sacrament of the Altar in this way, that what ever man has taken the order of the priesthood, be he never so vicious a man in his living, if he says duly the words over the bread that our Lord Jesus Christ said when he celebrated the Last Supper among his disciples where he sat at supper, I believe it is the his very flesh and his blood and not material bread and it cannot be unsaid once it has been said.")

Such an explicit answer makes the difference between Kempe and Sawtre extremely clear. While the mayor who hears this answer doubts her integrity—"'In fayth, sche menyth not wyth hir hert as sche seyd with hir mowthe'" (115:21–2) ("'In faith, she meant not with her heart as she said with her mouth'")—he alone is unconvinced. 'And þe clerjys seyden to hym, "Sir, sche answeryth ryth wel to vs"' (115:24) ('And the clerks said to him, "Sir, she answers very well to this."')

So it is, with this sense of Kempe's obedience to the structures of the Church clearly established for the reader, that we are prepared for the story of the bear. In the presence of the archbishop and his retinue, accused of anti-clericalism,

Kempe again tells the tale for which she has been indicted. The tide of public opinion at this gathering, hitherto running against her, is completely turned by the tale. The archbishop commends it, and the cleric who initiated its retelling undergoes a spiritual sea-change: "'Ser, þis tale smytyth me to þe hert'" (127:37–8). Kempe receives a paid escort to her next destination. This incident in the *Book* carries marks of an exemplary tale in a number of significant ways. Marked as 'narracio,' the tale of the priest and the pear tree validates Kempe's experience in the context of the *Book* as a treatise of contemplation, one which, ironically, could work without the intervention of priests. What happens to her serves as a salutary example in the metatext of the *Book*: there is spiritual illumination for the reader here.

Within the tale is a complex of relationships between Kempe as an agent and the figures of authority against which she is so often described as being pitted. Negotiating the highly problematic space in which she was located, as devout laywoman, Kempe figures both as teller of the tale and within the tale. Ingeniously, she invites readings that serve to predetermine the responses the tale receives, just as she does by refusing to justify herself to the mayor, and instead speaks in confession to the clergy, in chapter 48.[17] Here, the 'doctowr,' for example, is figured in the *narracio* as the ignorant and wayward priest who needs to be told twice before getting the message. On first hearing, the tale for him has been anti-clerical. Once the tale is retold, just as the priest has the tale interpreted for him, he understands his error. The necessary interpreter for the priest is the pilgrim/palmer, for the cleric it is Kempe. The identification between pilgrim/palmer and Kempe is established in the phrase 'schewyng hym-selfe þe messenger of God' (127:14–15) which precedes the pilgrim's interpretation. The assembly and the reader are invited to make the association between Kempe and the pilgrim as instruments of divine revelation.

The core of the tale, however, is susceptible to an analysis that defends the rôle of the clergy, through providing and glossing a negative exemplum. A story that focuses on the misbehaviour of one priest highlights the importance of the function he performs. By emphasising the inadequacy of one unnamed, hypothetical priest represented negatively as behaving 'as it wer a man of þe world' (127:25), the correct gap between priest and people is restored and reinforced.

The ambiguities of this story, its double-edgedness, are symptomatic of Kempe's position as laywoman in a culture that preferred its religious women enclosed. At the beginning of the story Kempe's narrative is marked with disclaimers of the charge that her story is anti-clerical. Rather than the tales of priests that she is accused of telling, she says she 'spak but of o preste be þe menner of exampyl' (126:24–5). The story does not pertain to the generality of the clergy and is told for spiritual illumination rather than from malicious intent. Furthermore, the hand of God is evident, as the priest became lost in the wood 'thorw þe sufferawns of God for þe profite of hys sowle' (126:26–7). Here the disclaimers and disavowals mark Kempe as medium or vehicle as the pilgrim in the tale is later to be seen. The message sanctions the medium here in a way familiar, often as an explicit strategy, to other medieval women such as Hildegard of Bingen, whose considerable talents could safely find expression as a manifestation from God.

Unresolvable contradictions circulate around Kempe and the story she tells. On the one hand, the story supports the idea that the clergy have a particularly important rôle in receiving the communion for the people in a period that Bynum identified as imbuing the consecration of the sacraments with increased significance. The construction of the rood screen to physically separate priest and altar from the congregation, the celebration of the mass by a priest 'with his back to the people, reciting the canon of the mass in an inaudible whisper,'[18] and the shift in focus from the moment of communion to that of consecration, entail fundamentally different relations between church and people.

> By the thirteenth century the eucharist, once a communal meal that bound Christians together and fed them with the comfort of heaven, had become an object of adoration....Since Christ arrived at the moment of consecration, not of communion, he arrived in the hands of the priest before he appeared on the tongue of the individual believer.[19]

The description of the priest who abuses his position in taking 'ful lytyl heede how þu seyst þi Makeynes and þi Seruyse, so it be blaberyd to an ende' (127:18–19) validates the notion of the priest's special rôle. Here, the bear-like priest fails to fulfil the rôle explicated by Kempe in her account of the Sacrament of the Altar, that he 'sey dewly þo wordys ouyr þe bred þat owr Lord Ihesu Criste seyde whan he mad hys Mawnde a-mong hys disciplys þer he sat at þe soper' (115:13–15). It is Kempe's duty to rehearse the importance of the priest through chastising those who err. While the reprimand issued by the uneducated lay voices of the pilgrim and Kempe implicitly questions the notion that the priest is the only divinely authorised vehicle for education, neither of them questions the significance of the sacraments that the priest alone can dispense.

Time and time again, Kempe confirms this in her *Book*. Repeatedly she tells of regularly taking communion, even while on pilgrimages in Rome and elsewhere.[20] Slandered by a priest in Rome, ejected from the Hospital of St Thomas of

Canterbury, where she has been used to making confession and receiving communion, it is her inability to continue to do so that is the result of the priest's 'euyl,' and is the source of her lament (80:17).

On the other hand, she also sees evidence of the consecration of the Sacraments when the ritual is carried out properly.

> On a day as þis creatur was heryng hir Messe, a ʒong man and a good prest heldyng up þe Sacrament in hys handys ouyr hys hed, þe Sacrament schok and flekeryd to & fro as a dowe flekeryth wyth hir wengys. &, whan he held up þe chalys wyth þe precyows Sacrament, þe chalys mevyd to & fro as it xuld a fallyn owt of hys handys. (47:15–21)

> (One day when this creature was hearing Mass, a young man and a good priest, holding up the Sacrament in his hands over his head, the Sacrament shook and fluttered to and fro as a dove flutters its wings and, when he held up the chalice with the precious Sacrament, the chalice moved to and fro as if it would have fallen out of his hands.)

And again, while many things remind Kempe of the reverence due to Christ, this occurs 'most of alle whan sche sey þe precyows Sacrament born a-bowte þe town wyth lyts & reuerns, þe pepil kenlyng on her kneys' (172:29–31) ('most of all when she saw the precious Sacrament carried around the town with lights and reverence, the people kneeling on their knees.')

Lochrie's study of Kempe argues that 'the success of Kempe's tale lies not only in its scatological subject but in its rhetoric of defilement....The near pun of the bear's *tayl* and Kempe's *tale* render the "voiding" of one equivalent to the telling of the other.'[21] While it is tempting, particularly from a contemporary feminist perspective, to see Kempe as involved in a carnivalesque act that is partly a rejection of masculinist church authorities, the textual context of the incident also needs to be remembered. The proem to the text is printed at the head of the Meech and Allen EETS edition and the Penguin translation by B. A. Windeatt, while the first translation by Butler-Bowdon in 1936 marginalised the proem to an appendix. The extracts published in 1501 and 1521 follow the proem in declaring themselves part of 'A shorte treatyse of contemplacyon taught by our lorde Ihesu cryste' (xlvi). A key element in the proem, however, which has an increased significance in being placed before the main text of the *Book*, is the directive to the reader, indicating the purpose of the text.

> Here begynnth a schort tretys and a comfortabyl for synful wrecchys, wher-in þei may haue gret solas and comfort to hem and vndyrstondyn þe hy and vnspecabyl mercy of ower souereyn Sauyowr Cryst Ihesu, whos name be worschepd and magnyfyed wythowten ende....(1:1–5)

(Here begins a short treatise and a comfortable one for sinful wretches wherein they may have great solace and comfort for themselves and understand the high and inexpressible mercy of our sovereign saviour Christ Jesus, whose name be worshipped and magnified without end.)

In this context, Kempe's story of the bear, the priest, and the pear tree can be seen, more consistently, as demonstrating Christ's mercy and grace than Kempe's rebelliousness.

While I am not arguing that the framing proem can or should completely determine readings of the text that follows, there are, it seems to me, dangers in focussing on the subversive elements and reading *The Book of Margery Kempe* as a realist text. What kind of relationship the incident involving Kempe and Henry Bowet had to reality is debatable, as Collis noted,[22] and in the end unlikely ever to be determinable. The incident in the narrative does, however, fulfil exactly the same function as the tale of the priest and the pear tree in that it demonstrates 'þe hy and vnspecabyl mercy of ower souereyn Savyowr Cryst Ihesu' (1:3–4). The fallen priest is redeemed; the doctor is corrected, and Kempe is saved from further allegations of heresy and punishment in the archbishop's court. In the context of the *Book*, the events of Kempe at York illustrate the providence of God in inspiring and protecting his 'creature.'

Lochrie locates the 'scatologic humor' 'in the text' and 'of the text as well,' yet precisely because this mocking laughter was pervasive 'in the medieval fabliau and in religious tales,'[23] it can also be seen as part of a tradition rather than peculiar to Kempe herself. To say this is not to diminish the sense of Kempe's agency but rather to re-locate it. The events of 1417 between Kempe and Bowet, recorded in the *Book*, are exemplary rather than realistic. Perhaps the events did unfold as Kempe suggests, perhaps not. In the *Book* we do have left to us, while we may not see Kempe laughing up her sleeve at members of the male church hierarchy, more importantly for Kempe, as the teller of the tales that are the *Book*, the incident is made to serve the purposes of self-validation. The end of the *capitulum* in which the priest and the pear tree appear announces the point of the incident in the narrative of the *Book*:

Than sche, goyng a-ȝen to ȝorke, was receyued of mech pepil and of ful worthy clerkys, whech enjoyed in owr Lord þat had ȝouyn hir not lettryd witte and wisdom to answeryn so many lernyd men wyth-owtyn velani or blame, thankyng be to God. (128:26–31)

(Then she, going again to York, was received by many people and very worthy clerks who rejoiced in our Lord who had given her, not an educated person, wit and wisdom to answer so many learned men without shame or disgrace, thanks be to God.)

In the next *capitulum* Kempe is arrested again and imprisoned in Beverley; the dark night of the soul, the pilgrim's struggle against earthly exigencies continues and validates Kempe as abused on earth, therefore, valued in heaven.

Furthermore, in the context of the whole chapter, the bear story replicates a pattern of explanation and conversion. At the beginning of the section when Kempe is publicly abused, reviled as Lollard and heretic, we see the first instance of conversion through the power of speech, through divine aid. To the threat that she should be burnt at the stake for heresy, Kempe replies with her own threats of fire.

> 'Serys, I drede me ʒe xul be brent in helle wyth-owtyn ende les ʒoan ʒe amende ʒow of ʒowr othys sweryng, for ʒe kepe not þe comawndementys of God. I wolde not sweryn as ʒe don for al þe good of þis worlde.' (124:4–7)

> ('Sirs, I fear that you shall be burnt in hell without end unless you correct yourselves of your oath-swearing, because you do not keep God's commandments. I would not swear as you do for all the wealth in the world.')

Then, for the first time in this chapter we see the pattern of conversion that the bear story rehearses. 'Þan þei ʒedyn a-wey as þei had ben a-schamyd' (124:7–8). (Then they went away as if they were ashamed.)

On the other side of the bear story we see the same pattern of accusation, reply and conversion. As if the parable had not made the message plain enough, Kempe spells it out even more directly to the miserable clerk who initially accused her.

> The forseyd creatur seyd to þe clerk, 'A, worschipful doctowr, ser, in place wher my dwellyng is most, is a worthy clerk, a good prechar, whech boldly spekyth ageyn þe mysgouernawns of þe pepil & wil flatyr no man. He seyth many tymes in þe pulpit, "ʒyf any man be euyl plesyd wyth my prechyng, note hym wel, for he is gylty." And ryth so, ser,' seyd sche to þe clerk, 'far ʒe be me, God forʒeve it ʒow.' (127–8)

> (The foresaid creature said to the clerk, 'A worshipful doctor, sir, in the place where I mostly live, is a worthy clerk and a good preacher, who boldly speaks against the misconduct of the people and will flatter no one. He says many times in the pulpit "if any man is displeased with my preaching, note him well, for he is guilty." 'And right so, sir,' she said to the clerk, 'fare you by me, God forgive you.')

Not surprisingly 'Þe clerk wist not wel what he myth sey to hir' (128:7–8) ('The clerk did not well know what to say to her'), although he has absorbed the message to the extent that he comes to her later and prays for her forgiveness for being against her. Yet again, we see the accusation, reply, conversion pattern that the story demonstrates. In all three cases, too, the significance of the religious lay observer is emphasised as goad and moral conscience.

The repetition of the same features and elements in the stories, in turn, suggests the deliberate construction of material, which takes on a shape and design not perceptible to the characters within it. The accumulation or variation on a theme are only appreciated by the careful and attentive reader, focussed on the book as a 'schort tretys' (1:1), demonstrating divine grace to be seen 'yf lak of charyte be not ower hynderawnce' (1:9–10) ('if lack of charity is not a hinderance'). In turn, this suggests a shaper and constructor as Sue Ellen Holbrook has argued.[24]

Throughout the *Book* Kempe is accused, and abused, puts her story, and the accusers sees the error of their ways. As Holbrook has argued, this is evident in the account of how the *Book* came to be written. The obstacles and hinderances in the recording of Kempe's words partly involve the initial inability of the priest and putative scribes to understand, believe, and even see the truth of Kempe's position. They have to confront their own error first. So, too, the overdressed Bishop of Worcester's men, whom Kempe describes as "'lykar þe Deuelys men'" (109:16) ("'more like the devil's men'"), in response initially 'weryn wroth and chedyn hir & spokyn angrily vn-to hir' (109:16–17) ('were angry and chided her, and spoke angrily to her'). However, when 'sche spak so sadly a-geyn syn & her mysgouernawns' ('she spoke so sadly against sin and their misconduct'), we see again the pattern of conversion: 'þei wer in sylens & held hem wel plesyd wyth hyr dalyawns' (109:18–20) ('they were silent and held themselves well pleased with her conversation').[25] And, again, in the story that Kempe tells about seeing herself as the butt of a joke going around London with which I began this book, it is she who has the last laugh. While they have mocked her presumed hypocrisy in the choice of food, she reminds them of the dangers of loose speaking: "'ʒe awt to seyn no wers þan ʒe knowyn and ʒet not so euyl as ʒe knowyn'" (244:35–6). In turn, the reproved diners repeat the experience of so many before them. 'Whan þei beheldyn hir not meyd in þis mater, no-thyng repreuyng hem, desiryng thorw þe spirit of charite her correccyon, [þei] wer rebukyd of her owyn honeste, obeyng hem to a-seeth makyng' (245:3–7). ('When they saw that she was not moved in the matter, not reproving them, desiring their correction in the spirit of charity, they were rebuked by her honesty, humbling themselves to make amends.')[26]

This kind of approach, focussing on the repetition of certain patterns of conversion and the establishment of fundamental religious beliefs by Kempe, allows us to distinguish more clearly between a Kempe and a William Sawtre, between orthodoxy and Lollardy. As Rodney Hilton aptly put it, not all public disorder is seen as threatening by established authorities. Kempe, far from challenging 'the relations of production which are at the heart of the social order,'[27] can be seen as supporting them in the context of the *Book* as a whole. Sawtre, on the other hand, did challenge the relations of production at the heart of the Catholic church. His public statements against transubstantiation voice dissension from within the body of the church, diminishing the rôle of the priest and the authority of church leaders. He threatens the rôle of the clergy as mediators between people and God. Recognised as a threat, he is removed. Kempe validates church authority and in doing so obtains free passage, albeit one that has to be continuously re-negotiated. *The Book of Margery Kempe* is both an account, accurate or otherwise, of these negotiations between devout laywoman and male church authorities and a negotiation for spiritual immortality itself. As an account of Kempe's spiritual struggles, the *Book* is the major card in Kempe's bid for the acceptance of her life as in *imitatio Christi*.

The story of the bear can be seen as more suggestive of a fundamental orthodoxy than either Lochrie or Staley attribute to the passage, the book, and Kempe herself. One way of accounting for the fact that Kempe lived to tell her tale is that she was not seen as challenging conventions.[28] Indeed, in many ways she can be seen as confirming them. By launching into the bear story, Kempe is certainly linking into a controversial subject as Sawtre's death indicated and as Bynum's analysis suggests. Staley argues well the significance of this in terms of contemporary debates. However, the attack on Kempe as Lollard and heretic is part of a much broader perception of mystics as Atkinson suggests.

> Mystics in any period are vulnerable to charges of heresy and disobedience, because their direct communication with God tends to bypass the services and sacraments of the Church.[29]

The bear story indicates precisely how careful Kempe was to avoid this accusation in a story of her own devising, which positions her as defender of the Mass and its servants.

An analysis of the story of the bear and the interpretations that it has received reveals much about the shifting fashions of cultural criticism. It is not simply significant for what it tells us about the importance of the Eucharist, as the Benedictine suggests, but neither can it really be taken as evidence of Kempe's carnivalesque rebelliousness, even given the scatological feel of the story. It provides a fascinating example of the dialogues between text and critics, the layering of interpretations over time, and of criticism as process. Furthermore, as a narrative, it manifests the power of story-telling, which has provoked so much interest since the fifteenth century both within and about *The Book of Margery Kempe*.

Notes

1. Karma Lochrie notes one possible analogue from medieval sermon material discussed by G. R. Owst, *Literature and the Pulpit in Medieval England* (Oxford: Basil Blackwell, 1961), p. 454, but the key elements for my discussion, the bear, the priest, and the pear-tree, are missing. See *Margery Kempe and Translations of the Flesh* (Philadelphia: University of Pennsylvania Press, 1991), pp. 164–5, fn. 18.

2. For further discussion of these annotations, see Meech and Allen's EETS volume, pp. xxxv–xlv.

3. A Benedictine of Stanbrook, 'Margery Kempe and the Holy Eucharist,' *The Downside Review*, 56, 1938, pp. 468–82.

4. Ibid., p. 482.

5. Karma Lochrie, op. cit., pp. 9 & 10.

6. Ibid., p. 149.

7. Ibid., p. 136.

8. As Karma Lochrie notes, Martin Thornton was one of the few scholars whom she knew to have discussed humour in relation to the book as a whole. It is also something that Allen noted in her papers in Bryn Mawr College Archives.

9. This tension in Lochrie's analysis, between being informed by contemporary debates in theory and the problems of ahistoricism, can also be seen and is addressed in 'The Language of Transgression: Body, Flesh, and Word in Mystical Discourse,' ed. Allen J. Frantzen, *Speaking Two Languages* (Albany: State University of New York Press, 1991), where she suggests that while it is 'neither desirable nor feasible for scholars of medieval mysticism to adopt this language of abjection, it is possible for us to try to describe its practices,' p. 138.

10. Lynn Staley, *Margery Kempe's Dissenting Fictions* (Pennsylvania: The Pennsylvania State University Press, 1994).

11. Ibid., pp. 10 & 9.

12. See Rufus M. Jones, *Studies in Mystical Religion* (London: Macmillan & Co. Ltd, 1909) and Clarissa W. Atkinson, *Mystic and Pilgrim: The Book and the World of Margery Kempe* (Ithaca: Cornell University Press, 1983).

13. Rufus M. Jones, op. cit., p. 361. Sawtre here presages other early materialists such as the sixteenth-century miller Menochio, who disputed the virgin birth because of his lived experience: "'I based my belief on the fact that many men have been born into the world, but none of a virgin woman,'" Carlo Ginsburg, *The Cheese and the Worms: The Cosmos of a Sixteenth-Century Miller*, tr. John and Anne Tedeschi (London: Routledge and Kegan Paul, 1980). p. 28.

14. Caroline Walker Bynum, *Holy Feast and Holy Fast: The Religious Significance of Food to Medieval Women* (Berkeley: University of California Press, 1987), p. 58. See also Eamon Duffy, *The Stripping of the Altars: Traditional Religion in England 1400-1580* (New Haven: Yale University Press, 1992), pp. 109–110.

15. Ibid., p. 57.

16. See Meech and Allen, 1940, 36: 20–24 and 61: 4–8.

17. See chapter 6 for my discussion of this incident.

18. Caroline Walker Bynum, op. cit., p. 56.

19. Ibid., p. 53.

20. See, for example, 65: 38–9, & 80: 10.

21. Karma Lochrie, op. cit., p. 150.

22. See chapter 6 for a discussion of Collis' treatment of the story in her text *The Apprentice Saint*.

23. Karma Lochrie, op. cit., pp. 151, 136 & 151.

24. Sue Ellen Holbrook, "'About Her": Margery Kempe's Book of Feeling and Working,' *The Idea of Medieval Literature* (Newark: University of Delaware Press, 1992), pp. 265–284.

25. This incident is also discussed in chapter 6 above.

26. See chapter 1 for a fuller analysis of this scene from a different perspective.

27. Rodney Hilton, *Class Conflict and the Crisis of Feudalism* (London: Verso, 1990), p. 80.

28. Clarissa W. Atkinson, op. cit., also argues that Kempe's social status contributed to her safe passage, pp. 78–9.

29. Ibid., p. 103.

Chapter 8

Re-Reading *The Book of Margery Kempe*

The history of *The Book of Margery Kempe*, from the time it was written to its reproductions in the present day, is a record of conflict and struggle. As a document of a would-be saint, it records the physical, emotional, and ideological struggles of a fifteenth-century woman who presents a narrative of her life to illuminate the religious path for others and for herself. In the descriptions of battling an uxorious husband, pleasure-seeking pilgrims, and those who simply accost her by throwing water over her or otherwise laying hands on her, the *Book* illustrates the trials and tribulations of a pilgrim's progress. The success of her quest lies partially in the physical existence of the manuscript itself, which is a testament to her powers of persuasion, not least over the initially reluctant and inadequate scribes. The manuscript represents the success of Kempe's battles and is a material manifestation of Kempe's ability to convert her contemporaries to her side. Even in the last pages of the second book, we are reminded both of the struggles that characterise her story and of her success in overcoming the manifold obstacles that continually confronted her. Her confessor 'ȝaf hir ful scharp wordys, for sche was hys obediencer and had takyn vp-on hir swech a jurne wyth-owten hys wetyng' ('spoke to her sharply, for she owed him obedience and had undertaken a journey without his knowledge'), criticising her for undertaking the journey to Calais without his permission. He, like many others before him, 'was meuyd þe mor a-geyn hir,' until, with 'halpe' from 'owr Lord,' 'sche had as good loue of hym & of oþer frendys aftyr as sche had be-forn' (247: 24–9) ('she had as much love from him and other friends as she had had before.'). Both the struggle and the ability to effect change demonstrate the success of the *Book*. The production of the *Book* replicates the patterns of persuasion and conversion through which it came into being.

One powerful image, presented to Kempe as an account of how others work on her, can also be taken as a description of how she, literally, works on others, capturing the sense of labour that her story entails. In chapter 18, Kempe complains to the anchor of the Friar Preachers in Lynn that her confessor still deals with her sharply in spite of the fact that others like Julian of Norwich, whom she has just visited, believe her to be honestly inspired. The anchor explains to her the rôle of the confessor in an image that stands as a metaphor of her struggles through the *Book* as well as a metaphor of the effects she has on others. So the friction Kempe experiences, and the social friction of which she is the cause, can be seen to have the same effect in the life of the *Book*.

> 'God for ʒowr meryte hath ordeyned hym to be ʒowr scorge & faryth wyth ʒow as a smyth wyth a fyle þat makyth þe yron to be bryte & cler to þe sygth whech be-forn aperyd rusty, dryke, [&] euyl colowryd. Þe mor scharp þat he is to ʒow, [þe mor] clerly schinyth ʒowr sowle in þe sygth of God….'(44: 30–5)

> ('God for your merit has ordained him to be your scourge and deal with you as a smith does with a file that makes iron bright and clear to the sight that before appeared rusty, dark and evil-coloured. The more sharp he is with you [the more] clearly your soul shines in the sight of God….')

Kempe is thus filed and filer in an image that well captures the labour and effort of her endeavours with secular and religious powers, against which she endlessly asserts herself. It is the friction that produces the shiny soul.

This image can also be taken as a metaphor of the relationship between a cultural materialist approach and *The Book of Margery Kempe* itself. On the face of it *The Book of Margery Kempe* is an unlikely case for cultural materialism. Given the connections with marxism and feminism evident in cultural materialism, a book that is avowedly religious and concerned with life beyond the material might seem an unlikely choice. As a text it cannot be mined for evidence of class struggle nor dissected to reveal a proto-feminist conveniently foreshadowing the triumphs over adversity and opposition that have been so much a part of the context of modern feminism. The *Book* tests the resources of an approach whose aims and understandings it cannot reflect back to it. In this context, a cultural materialist approach might also be said to bring to such a text a certain amount of friction. Like the file in the hands of the smith, it might illuminate what sits beneath the surface, suggesting new shapes and outlines.

Cultural materialism refuses the idea that the rôle of the critic is to engage in the task of interpreting a text through an understanding of the mind of the author. Its trajectory is not a focussing in on the self that the text reveals but rather a movement to and from the text and the contexts and cultures within which it is inscribed. The recent reproductions of parts or the whole of *The Book of Margery Kempe* reposition both the book and person in divergent ways as I have argued in previous chapters. Part of the problem of searching for the author through the words on the page is the construction of a homogenous, monolithic voice that might actually deafen us to the multiple voices murmuring within and around the text. In the specific context of the *Book*, while there has been significant discussion of the effectiveness of distinguishing between Kempe and scribes and between Margery as a character and Kempe as 'author,' there has not been much discussion of the different kinds of voices perceptible in Book I, Book II, and the prayers. What seem to be distinctions, in particular, between character and author, nevertheless focus on a relationship that inevitably leads back to the author as controller of meaning in the kind of relationship identified by Foucault as analogous to a religious imperative.

Listening with an ear to the different kinds of voices within the text, other kinds of distinctions are audible, and they are susceptible to an analysis that foregrounds context, genre, and register. These distinctions also heighten the sense of differences within *The Book of Margery Kempe* and of the *Book* as process. In the first book, while we can hear differences between scribe and Kempe, as John C. Hirsh and Sue Ellen Holbrook have argued,[1] there is nevertheless a strong sense of the person called Margery Kempe. Precisely the things that some critics saw as denying Kempe the right to be taken seriously in religious terms testify to the strength and colour of her presence. In spite of what now appears as the quaintness of early critics' appreciation of Kempe's Englishness, they were right to identify the effectiveness of the *Book*'s use of language. Many of the phrases and images are redolent of a spontaneous appreciation of the world. So Kempe's God reassures her that the perils of hell and purgatory are not for her, but that 'whan þow schalt passyn owt of þis world, wyth-in þe twynkelyng of an eye þow schalt haue þe blysse of heuyn' (16: 37–17: 1) ('when you pass away out of this world within the twinkling of an eye you shall have the bliss of heaven'). Again, the image used to describe the length of time Kempe spends in conversation with God is simplicity itself and effective because of that: 'so her dalyawns contynuyd tyl sterrys apperyd in þe fyrmament' (37: 13–5) ('so her conversation continued until the stars appeared in the sky'). Her total obedience to God, in spite of the vicissitudes to which this exposes her, is again vibrantly described in her passionate declaration that 'ȝyf it wer thy wille, Lord, I wolde for þi lofe & for magnyfying of þi name ben hewyn as smal as flesch to þe potte' (142: 11–13) ('if it were your will, Lord, for your love and the magnifying of your name I would be chopped up as small as meat for the pot.')

While Book I has much in common with Book II, 'the continuation differs from the treatise in several ways.'[2] Both books employ a third-person narrative, different in effect and tone from the first-person presentations that are so much a feature of modern re-constructions of the text.[3] Yet there are differences in tone between the first book, and the second, beginning with the suggestion that it is the priest's own decision to continue the treatise after the completion of the first part. So he decides to do so, as he says, to include more evidence of what 'owr Lord wrowt in hys sympyl creatur ȝerys þat sche leuyd aftyr, not alle but summe of hem, aftyr hyr owyn tunge' (221: 10–12) ('our Lord brought about in his simple creature in the years after that she lived, not all of them but some of them, after her own words'). This third-person narrative has a quite different sense of being about someone than the one in the first book. Here the sense of 'aftyr' has much more the resonance of 'in the manner of,' suggesting imitation rather than dictation. What follows seems subtly different in style, with the incidents related being more distanced, more truncated, than the detailed descriptions and immediacy of the first book. This continuation seems produced with a sharper eye to the subordination of material that is secondary to the message. The account of the conversion of Kempe's son encapsulates the way in which the material is shaped with the end in mind, with the omission of comment not germane to the recounting of the son's repentance. The account is less affective than didactic. So, too, it is significant that while there are many uses of the word 'modyr' in Book I, this is most often to relation to Christ's mother or even the 'modyr' of the priest who reads to Kempe (143). Only in Book II is Kempe's rôle as mother made more apparent through the repeated application of the word to Kempe in the account of the son's conversion. The narrative here is a less evocative, more formal account of significant events. It is in the spirit of Book I rather than continuous with it. Even though Kempe is repeatedly represented in Book I by the phrase 'this creatur,' this is more circumlocution than communicative of a real sense of one person describing events happening to another. The immediacy of the experiences and feelings so evident in the first book is absent from the second as initiated by the priest.

Similarly, the description of the incident in which Kempe finds herself the butt of the joke about her passing off preferences for good food as self-denial, while characteristic of the episodes and vignettes that stud the first book, reflects a stronger sense of mediation. In Book I the descriptions of Kempe's tribulations tend to end in reinforcement of the positive point of Kempe's effectiveness in converting the abusers to proper reverence for God. In this second book there is an editorial aside about the status of the abusers that seems much more priest than Kempe: 'Þei wer fowndyn of þe Deuyl, fadyr of lesyngys, fauowryd, maynteynd, and born forth of hys membys, fals jnvyows pepil, hauyng indignacyon at hir vertuows leuyng, not of powyr to hyndryn hir but þorw her fals tungys' (243: 26–30) ('They were inventions of the devil, father of lies, favoured, maintained and born of his members, false envious people, having indignation at her virtuous living, powerless to hinder her except though their lying tongues.'). This seems the perspective of a partisan commentator providing an overview for the reader. Someone familiar with Kempe's life summarises from a distance.

In stark contrast with this stronger sense of mediation that is perceptible in Book II are the prayers with which the manuscript ends. Here, indeed, Kempe is represented through the first-person pronoun, as nowhere else in the text. It is, of course, still mediated by the words of the priest—'Whan sche had seyd "Veni creator spritus" wyth þe versys, sche seyd on þis maner' (248: 14–16) ('When she had said the "Veni creator spiritus" with all the verses belong to it, she said in this manner')—but the rest of the section is a first-person, direct articulation of words between Kempe and God. Whereas the first book concentrates on revelations of God to Kempe and her attempts to live through the consequences of that, here Kempe reveals to God her understandings in a way unprecedented in the other sections of the manuscript. The genre of the prayer form entails a quite different sense of voice to the description of a life in *imitatio christi*. Perhaps this is most clear in one particular sentence in the prayers that is both suggestive of other sources[4] and peculiar to *The Book of Margery Kempe*. At twenty-seven lines in the EETS edition, it is clearly the longest sentence in the text and is sustained by the driving force of Kempe's appreciation of how inadequate she or anything is to the task of thanking God for his mercy to her. The speech is an accumulation of imagery and ideas whose intent is to emphasise the obligations of the person, whose articulacy is contradictorily attested in the act of proclaiming inadequacy. The resonance of this sentence is quite apart from anything seen elsewhere in the text.

> Here my preyeris, for, þow I had as many hertys & sowlys closyd in my sowle as God knew wythowtyn begynnyng how many xulde dwellyn in Heuyn wythowtyn ende & as þer arn dropys of watyr, fres and salt, cheselys of grauel, stonys smale & grete, gresys growyng in al erthe, kyrnellys of corn, fischys, fowelys, bestys & leevys up-on treys whan moste plente ben, fedir of fowle er her of best, seed þat growith in erbe, er in wede, in flowyr, in lond, er in watyr whan most growyn, & as many creaturys as in erth han ben &

arn er xal ben myth ben be þi myth, and as þer arn sterrys & awngelys in þi syght er oþer
kynnes good þat growyth up-on erthe, & eche wer a sowle as holy as euyr was our Lady
Seynt Mary bar Ihesu owr Sauyowr, &, yf it wer possibyl þat eche cowde thynkyn &
spekyn al so gret reuerens & worschep as euyr dede owr Lady Seynt Mary her in erthe
and now doth in Heuyn & xal don wythowtyn ende, I may rith wel thynkyn in myn hert
& spekyn it wyth my mowth as þis tyme in worschip of þe Trinite & of al þe cowrt of
Heuyn, to gret schame and schenschep of Sathanas þat fel fro Goddys face & of alle hys
wikkyd spiritys, þat alle þes hertys ne sowlys cowde neuyr thankyn God ne ful preysyn
hym, ful blissyn hym ne ful worschepyn hym, ful louyn hym ne fully ȝeuyn lawdacyon,
preisyng, & reuerens to hym as he were worthy to han for þe gret mercy þat he hath
schewyd to me in erth þat I can not don ne may don. (251: 39–252: 27).

('Hear my prayers, for though I had as many hearts and souls closed in my soul as God
knew without beginning how many should dwell in heaven without end, and as there are
drops of water, fresh and salt, pebbles of gravel, stones small and large, grasses growing
on all the earth, kernels of corn, fish, fowls, beasts and leaves on the trees when they are
most abundant, feathers of fowls or hairs of beasts, seed that grows in plants, or in
weeds, in flowers, in land, or in water when most grow, and as many creatures as there
have ever been or ever shall be on the earth and might be through your power, and as
there are stars and angels in your sight or other kinds of good that grow on earth, and
each were a soul as holy as ever was our Lady Saint Mary who bore Jesus our Saviour,
and, if it were possible that each could think and speak such great reverence and worship
as ever our Lady Saint Mary did here on earth and now does in heaven and shall do
without end, I might right well think in my heart and speak it with my mouth as this time
in worship of the trinity and all the court of heaven, to the great shame and ignominy of
Satan who fell from God's sight and of all his wicked spirits, that all these hearts and
souls could not praise him nor fully worship him, fully loving him nor fully giving praise,
thanks and reverence to him as he were worthy of for the great mercy that he has shown
to me on earth, that I cannot do or may do.')

The concatenation of material objects, of concrete details, demonstrates the
triumph of the struggling soul in the presentation of a prayer or plea that is
both thanks and apology. It has the immediacy of imagery in Book I, where the
impact is achieved through an appeal to the ordinary, familiar, material objects
of the everyday world, whether it is stockfish or meat in the pot. In this
extraordinary sentence, Kempe envisages a world in microcosm, celebrating
infinite variety in an organised totality. It is an imaginative and imaginary vision
that marks the successful accomplishment of Margery Kempe's task of self-
sanctification. It is emblematic of the rhetorical strategies that are so
characteristic of the book. By this stage in the manuscript Kempe seems to
have earned the right to speak for herself and to use that voice to articulate a
plea that mercy be shown to 'alle my childeryn, gostly and bodily...alle my
frendys & alle myn enmijs' (251: 11–12, & 15–16) ('all my children, spiritual

and physical…all my friends and all my enemies'), in short, to everyone. Ironically, the singularity of the first-person pronoun announces the shift from self to the concern for the plight of others. The predominant concerns of the first book, in particular, were the treatment of self by others as a demonstration of humility and the direction of the self to the more than personal and mortal. Here we have a voice intent on pleading for others. The passage from Book I to the prayers is then the journey from scenes of personal confrontations to visions of global harmony.

From this perspective, while there can be seen to be 'books' of Margery Kempe in terms of the emphases and shapes that anthologies and editions give to the original text in the manuscript, it also seems that there is a plurality even in the original text that the modern title does not suggest. *The Book of Margery Kempe* is a treatise that contains two books and a series of prayers. It is more diverse, less homogenous and unified a textual commodity than has generally been perceived. The voices in the text are modulated to accomplish the different purposes that a particular section addresses, again manifesting the sense of the book as process, reflecting both the passage of Margery Kempe on her spiritual journey and that of the reader from spiritual exempla to spiritual affirmation.

The task for a political criticism like cultural materialism is not to identify and rescue texts reflective of its own politics but, as Alan Sinfield has argued, to 'observe how stories negotiate the faultlines that distress the prevailing conditions of plausibility.'[5] Political criticism, that is, needs to account for texts and events that stress or test out existing common understandings. The faultlines image is one which reverberates tellingly across the texts that both are and are not *The Book of Margery Kempe*. Earthquakes, lightning, thunder, rain, and snow often feature in the *Book* to illustrate Kempe's fear for her safety, her physical vulnerability, and her ability to survive. They also serve to demonstrate to others that Kempe has access to a higher authority than their good opinion or lack of it. The appearance or cessation of these natural forces serves as an indication of Kempe's authenticity. As God manifests himself at the moment in which the priest raises the shaking chalice at the altar, so this signifies, as he later explains to Kempe, an 'erdene' (47: 30) ('earthquake'), that he will send as punishment to the earth. Later on Kempe is also told that these 'thundirkrakkys…leuenys……wyndys…[and] erde-denys' (182:12,14,16 & 28) ('thundercracks…lightning…winds…[and] eathquakes') are manifestations of his disapproval of others, which Kempe is not to fear. Her interventions at these times of distress are then taken by her peers as miraculous evidence of her special position. Kempe operates as a kind of faultline in the *Book*, disturbing those around her but ultimately confirming the religious orthodoxies of her time.

In other ways, aside from the persona of Kempe herself, *The Book of Margery Kempe* has caused tremors of its own. Santha Bhattacharji's own attempt on the metaphor, *God Is an Earthquake: The Spirituality of Margery Kempe*,[6] is an intervention in a debate that for some has become too secularised, too political. So the foreword, by Sister Benedicta Ward SLG, to Bhattacharji's book asserts the need for a particular kind of stability to be returned to the *Book*. Here 'is the still, small voice of clarity, reason and discernment,' Ward argues, '[a]fter the earthquake of feminist examination.' This configuration not only confidently reasserts the authenticity of 'Margery's' mysticism but also sees it as 'providential' that the book was 'brought to light in the mid-twentieth century,' offering a new twist to the existing accounts of how and why the manuscript was identified.[7] Here feminism is the earthquake or faultline, rupturing the connections between past and present, thwarting the modern reader's identification with the mind of Kempe as revealed in the text.

The issue for cultural materialism, and the test it has to face, is whether it can respond to texts that do not share its assumptions without distorting them or re-writing them in its own image. My argument is that it can do this rather better than some discourses that have been applied to *The Book of Margery Kempe* and that it has much to contribute in the debates over its meanings, precisely because it has to recognise its differences from the text itself. The friction between text and theory produces new energy.

In the early twentieth century, among all the stories that were not *The Book of Margery Kempe*, one in particular stands out in terms of its own coincidence with that book. More than a decade before the identification of the Salthouse manuscript, Virginia Woolf wrote a story whose appearance uncannily presages *The Book of Margery Kempe*. Woolf's story has been given the title 'The Journal of Mistress Joan Martyn' and is told through the rather busy voice of a middle-aged female medieval historian, Miss Rosamond Merridew. Miss Merridew specialises in issues of land tenure in the thirteenth, fourteenth, and fifteenth centuries, and this leads her to seek out undiscovered manuscripts in old country houses—an event rather more common in the 1920s than it is now. So it is that she finds herself looking at just such a one.

> Here was one of those humble old Halls, then, which survive almost untouched, and
> practically unknown for centuries and centuries....This is the kind of place, I thought, as
> I stood with my hand on the bell, where the owners are likely to possess exquisite

manuscripts, and sell them as easily [to] the first rag man who comes along, as they would their pig wash, or the timber from the park.[8]

This fictional counterpart to Colonel Butler-Bowdon's Pleasington Old Hall also reveals a medieval manuscript of slightly later provenance than the *Book* but from the same area: "'The Journal of Mistress Joan Martyn...kept by her at Martyn's Hall, in the county of Norfolk the year of our Lord 1480.'"[9] This manuscript, unappreciated by its owners, is a journal, a direct record of Martyn's ideas and thoughts, particularly about her family relationships and her impending marriage to a neighbouring landowner. In content it is nothing like *The Book of Margery Kempe*, primarily because its concerns are secular and because it operates as a first-person narrative. It is very much the journal that a twentieth-century consciousness would make, far from the time when journal writing itself was an unknown genre. It is interesting, however, that such a story should precede the *Book*. No doubt inspired partly by books like the Paston letters, to which it directly refers,[10] the story attests to an interest in the lives of ordinary people in the medieval period. It provides, in a way, the imagined insights that F. M. Powicke and Christopher Morley requested when they wrote of reminiscences of women with 'the seeing eye for the fulcrum details on which the weights of life are swung.'[11] In its own way it demonstrates the felicitousness of *The Book of Margery Kempe*'s appearance. It is almost as if when it had not appeared by 1920, Virginia Woolf nearly had to invent it.

Yet by being so like and so unlike *The Book of Margery Kempe*, the story throws the *Book* into stark relief and returns to the *Book* the very strong sense that it is of its time, as the story is a story of its time. Woolf's tale is part of a series of tales in which she explores the consciousness of a female character. In this case the structure allows her to experiment with the consciousness of two female characters, Merridew, and Joan Martyn. Kempe's consciousness is quite other than either of these two modern counterparts, and Woolf's story shows that while the characters are supposed to be historically distant from each other, what connects them is the consciousness of their female creator.

Cultural materialism enables a broadening of the contexts into which *The Book of Margery Kempe* can be put such that different kinds of light can be shone on it, illuminating different kinds of meanings. Some of these contexts sharpen the sense of what the *Book* is, in terms of its original production, precisely by illustrating what it is not. It is not the journal of Mistress Joan Martyn nor the journal of Mistress Margery Kempe. Other contexts show how changes in language, format, physical appearance, and situational contexts radically alter what it is and what it does or means. There are now many books of Margery

Kempe, many contexts in which she appears, all of them subtly or substantially different from each other, produced by different kinds of people for different other people, with different kinds of purposes.

Through focussing on different situational contexts we can see how texts are made and re-made and with what effects. In the last seventy years, *The Book of Margery Kempe* has become increasingly important to medieval literature and to English Literature more generally, partly in spite of the religious content that was its original raison d'être. Both Kempe and the *Book* function as examples of an Englishness that is eccentric and quaint and is contradictorily positioned both as irremediably 'lost' and quintessentially timeless. Bundled from one cultural formation, one cultural production, to another, Kempe has been interrogated, psychoanalysed, examined, demonised, excluded, and sanctified. Yet at all of these moments the appearances of Kempe and the *Book* exemplify and reflect cultural criticism's changing interests and practices. If *The Book of Margery Kempe* was a 'chrysolite, of so many facets,' for *The Times* on October 10, 1936, then it has continued to be a jewel that reflects its own settings and the communities in which it is reproduced. As such, it is an important part of the making both of Middle English Literature and of English Literature in their scholarly and popular traditions.

Notes

1. John C. Hirsh, 'Author and Scribe in *The Book of Margery Kempe*,' *Medium Aevum*, 44, 1975, pp. 145–150; Sue Ellen Holbrook, '"About Her": Margery Kempe's Book of Feeling and Working,' *The Idea of Medieval Literature*, ed. James M. Dean and Christian K. Zacher (Newark: University of Delaware Press, 1992).

2. Sue Ellen Holbrook, '"About Her,"' p. 277. Holbrook concentrates on the differences in content.

3. See chapter 6 for a discussion of these modernisations.

4. Hope Emily Allen's note in the EETS text suggests connections to Suso's *Vita* and Corinthians.

5. Alan Sinfield, *Faultlines: Cultural Materialism and the Politics of Dissident Reading* (Oxford: Oxford University Press, 1992), p. 47.

6. Santha Bhattacharji, *God Is an Earthquake: The Spirituality of Margery Kempe* (London: Darton, Longman and Todd, 1997).

7. Ibid., p. xiii.

8. Virginia Woolf, '[The Journal of Mistress Joan Martyn],' *The Complete Shorter Fiction of Virginia Woolf*, ed. Susan Dick (London: Hogarth Press, 1985), pp. 36 & 36.

9. The story is unpolished and does include various inconsistencies, one of them being that while the journal is dated 1480, Martyn was supposed to be born in 1495.

10. Virginia Woolf also discusses the Pastons directly in her essay, 'The Pastons and Chaucer,' *The Common Reader*, Volume I, originally published in 1925, ed. Andrew McNeillie (London: The Hogarth Press, 1984).

11. Christopher Morley's review of Trevelyan's *English Social History* in Bryn Mawr College Archives without full reference. See chapter 2 for a fuller discussion.

Bibliography

Unpublished Material

B.L. Add. MS 61823, Bodleian Library, Oxford, UK.

Lynn Museum & Townhouse Museum papers, King's Lynn, Norfolk, UK.

MSS English Letters c. 212, d. 217 & d. 268, & MS. Engl. Misc. c. 484, Bodleian Library, Oxford, UK.

The Hope Emily Allen Papers, Bryn Mawr College Special Collections, Pennsylvania, USA.

The Joan Wake Papers, Northamptonshire Record Office, Northampton, UK.

Published Material

A Benedictine of Stanbrook. 1938. 'Margery Kempe and the Holy Eucharist,' *The Downside Review* 56: 468–82.

Aers, David, ed. 1985. *Medieval Literature: Criticism, Ideology and History*. Brighton: Harvester Press.

———1988a. *Community, Gender, and Individual Identity: English Writing 1360–1430*. London: Routledge.

———1988b. 'Rewriting the Middle Ages: Some Suggestions.' *The Journal of Medieval and Renaissance Studies* 18.2: 221–40.

Allen, Hope Emily. 1934. Letter to *The Times*, 27 December: 15.

———1935. 'The Three Daughters of Deorman.' *PMLA* 50: 899–902.

Ashley, Kathleen. 1998. 'Historicising Margery: *The Book of Margery Kempe* as Social Text,' *Journal of Medieval and Early Modern Studies* 28.2, Spring: 371–88.

Astell, Ann, ed. 2000. *Lay Sanctity, Medieval and Modern*. Notre Dame: University of Notre Dame Press.

Atkinson, Clarissa. 1983. *Mystic and Pilgrim: The Book and the World of Margery Kempe*. Ithaca: Cornell University Press.

Bacon, Alan, ed. 1998. *The Nineteenth Century History of English Studies*. Aldershot: Ashgate.

Bacon, Leonard. 1944. Rev. of *The Book of Margery Kempe 1436: A Modern Version* by W. Butler Bowdon. *Saturday Review of Literature*, 4 November: 12.

Beckwith, Sarah. 1986. 'A Very Material Mysticism: The Medieval Mysticism of Margery Kempe.' *Medieval Literature: Criticism, Ideology and History*. Ed. David Aers. Brighton: Harvester Press, 34–57.

———1993. *Christ's Body: Identity, Culture and Society in Late Medieval Writings*. London: Routledge.

———1992. 'Problems of Authority in Late Medieval English Mysticism: Language, Agency, and Authority in *The Book of Margery Kempe*.' *Exemplaria* 4.1, 171–99.

Bennett, Tony. 1990. *Outside Literature*. London: Routledge.

Berg, Maxine. 1996a. *A Woman in History: Eileen Power 1889–1940*. Cambridge: Cambridge University Press.

——— 1996b. 'Eileen Power: 1889–1940.' Eds. Edward Shils and Carmen Blacker. *Cambridge Women: Twelve Portraits*. Cambridge: Cambridge University Press.

Bhattacharji, Santha. 1997. *God Is an Earthquake: The Spirituality of Margery Kempe*. London: Darton, Longman & Todd.

Bloch, R. Howard & Stephen G. Nichols. 1996. *Medievalism and the Modernist Temper*. Baltimore: The Johns Hopkins University Press.

Bosse, Roberta Bux. 1979. 'Margery Kempe's Tarnished Reputation: A Reassessment.' *14thCentury English Mystics Newsletter* V.1: 9–19.

———1984. 'Female Sexual Behaviour in the Late Middle Ages: Ideal and Actual.' *Fifteenth-Century Studies* 10: 15–37.

Bradley, Marion. 1982. *The Mists of Avalon*. London: Sphere Books.

Brownlee, Marina S., Kevin Brownlee, and Stephen G. Nichols. 1991. *The New Medievalism*. Baltimore: The Johns Hopkins University Press.

Bynum, Caroline Walker. 1987. *Holy Feast and Holy Fast: The Religious Significance of Food to Medieval Women*. Berkeley: University of California Press.

Butler-Bowdon, W., ed. 1936. *The Book of Margery Kempe 1436: A Modern Version*. London: Jonathan Cape.

Cantor, Norman E. 1991. *Inventing the Middle Ages: The Lives, Works, and Ideas of the Great Medievalists of the Twentieth Century*. New York: William Morrow.

Chandler, Alice. 1971. *A Dream of Order: The Medieval Ideal in Nineteenth-Century English Literature*. London: Routledge and Kegan Paul.

Chomeley, Katherine. 1948. *Margery Kempe: Genius and Mystic*. London: The Catholic Book Club.

Coleman, T. W. 1938. *English Mystics of the Fourteenth Century*. London: Epworth Press.

Colledge, Edmund. 1985. Rev. of *Mystic and Pilgrim: The Book and the World of Margery Kempe* by Clarissa Atkinson. *Catholic Historical Review* 71.4: 647–650.

Collis, Louis. 1964. *The Apprentice Saint*. London: Michael Joseph. Rpt as *Memoirs of a Medieval Woman*. New York: Harper and Row, 1964.

Cottle, Basil. 1969. *The Triumph of English*. London: Blandford.

Crook, Paul. 1991. 'W. R. Inge and Cultural Crisis, 1899–1920.' *Journal of Religious History* 16.4: 410–32.

Dean, James M. & Christian K. Zacher. 1992. *The Idea of Medieval Literature: New Essays on Chaucer and Medieval Culture in Honor of Donald R. Howard*. Newark: University of Delaware Press.

Delany, Sheila. 1983. *Writing Woman*. New York: Schocken Books.

———1987. '"Mothers to Think Back Through": Who Are They? The Ambiguous Example of Christine de Pizan.' Ed. Laurie A. Finke and Martin B. Shichtman. *Medieval Texts and Contemporary Readers*. Ithaca: Cornell University Press, 177–129.

Derrida, Jacques. 1986. *Of Grammatology*. Trans. Gayatri Chakravorty Spivak. Baltimore: The Johns Hopkins University Press.

Devlin-Glass, Francis & Lyn McCredden, eds. 2001. *Feminist Poetics of the Sacred: Creative Suspicions*. Oxford: Oxford University Press.

Dinshaw, Carolyn. 1999. *Getting Medieval: Sexualities and Communities, Pre- and Postmodern*. Durham and London: Duke University Press.

Dinshaw, Carolyn & David Wallace, eds. 2003. *The Cambridge Companion to Medieval Women's Writing*. Cambridge: Cambridge University Press.

Dollimore, Jonathan & Alan Sinfield. 1985. *Political Shakespeare: New Essays in Cultural Materialism*. Manchester: Manchester University Press.

————1990. 'Culture and Texuality: Debating Cultural Materialism.' *Textual Practice* 4.1: 91–100.

Dollimore, Jonathan. 1988. 'The Dominant and the Deviant: A Violent Dialectic.' *Futures for English*. Manchester: Manchester University Press, 179–192.

Doob, Penelope B. R. 1974. *Nebuchadnezzar's Children: Conventions of Madness in Middle English Literature*. New Haven: Yale University Press.

Doody, Margaret Anne. 1988. *Frances Burney: The Life in the Works*. New Brunswick: Rutgers University Press.

Douglas, Mary. 1984. *Purity and Danger: An Analysis of the Concepts of Pollution and Taboo*. London: Ark Paperbacks.

Douie, D. L. 1937–8. Rev. of *The Book of Margery Kempe 1436: A Modern Version* by W. Butler-Bowdon. *History: The Quarterly Journal of the Historical Association*, ns. XXII: 70–2.

Duffy, Eamon. 1992. *The Stripping of the Altars: Traditional Religion in England 1400–1580*. New Haven: Yale University Press.

Dyhouse, Carol. 1995. *No Distinction of Sex: Women in British Universities, 1870–1939*. London: UCL Press.

Eagleton, Mary. 1990. *Feminist Literary Theory: A Reader*. Oxford: Blackwell.

Eggert, Paul. 1990. *Editing in Australia*. Occasional Paper 17. Canberra: University College, Australian Defence Force Academy.

Erskine, John A. 1989. 'Margery Kempe and Her Models: The Role of the Authorial Voice.' *Mystics Quarterly* 15.6: 75–85.

Finke, Laurie A. & Martin B. Shichtman. 1987. *Medieval Texts and Contemporary Readers*. Ithaca: Cornell University Press.

Fish, Stanley. 1980. *Is There a Text in This Class?* Cambridge, Mass.: Harvard University Press.

————1989. *Doing What Comes Naturally*. Oxford: Clarendon Press.

Fox-Genovese, Elizabeth. 1991. *Feminism Without Illusions: A Critique of Individualism*. Chapel Hill: University of North Carolina Press.

Foucault, Michel. 1977. *Language, Counter-Memory, Practice*. Ed. Donald F. Bouchard, trans. Sherry Simon. Ithaca: Cornell University Press.

Frantzen, Allen J. 1990. *Desire for Origins: New Language, Old English and Teaching the Tradition*. New Brunswick: Rutgers University Press.

————,ed. 1991. *Speaking Two Languages: Traditional Disciplines and Contemporary Theory in Medieval Studies*. Albany, New York: State University of New York Press.

————1993. 'When Women Aren't Enough.' *Speculum* 68: 445–71.

Gallyon, Margaret. 1995. *Margery Kempe of Lynn and Medieval England*. Norwich: The Canterbury Press.

Ganim, John M. 1996. "The Myth of Medieval Romance,' *Medievalism and the Modern Temper*. Ed. R. Howard Bloch & Stephen G. Nichols. Baltimore: The Johns Hopkins University Press.

Gardner, Edmund G., ed. 1966. *The Cell of Self-Knowledge: Seven Early English Mystical Treatises Printed by Henry Pepwell in 1521*. New York: Cooper Square.

Garnham, Nicholas. 1983. 'Towards a Theory of Cultural Materialism.' *Journal of Communication* 33.3: 314–329.

Gilbert, Sandra & Susan Gubar, eds. 1996. *The Norton Anthology: Literature by Women: The Traditions in English.* New York: W. W. Norton & Co.

Ginsburg, Carlo. 1980. *The Cheese and the Worms: The Cosmos of a Sixteenth-Century Miller.* trans. John and Anne Tedeschi. London: Routledge & Kegan Paul.

Glenn, Cheryl. 1992. 'Author, Audience and Autobiography: Rhetorical Technique in *The Book of Margery Kempe.*' *College English* 54.5: 540–553.

Glück, Robert. *Margery Kempe.* 1994. New York: High Risk Books/Serpent's Tail.

Goggin, Jacqueline. 1992. 'Challenging Sexual Discrimination in the Historical Profession: Women Historians and the American Historical Association, 1890–1940.' *The American Historical Review* 97.3.

Goldberg, Jonathan. 1997. *Desiring Women Writing: English Renaissance Examples,* Stanford, California: Stanford University Press, 1977.

Goodman, Antony E. 1978. The Piety of John Brunham's Daughter of Lynn.' Ed. Derek Baker. *Medieval Women.* Oxford: Blackwell, 347–358.

Gordon, Peter. 1992. *The Wakes of Northampton: A Family History.* Northampton: Northamptonshire Libraries and Information Service.

Gray, Douglas, ed. 1985. *The Oxford Book of Medieval Prose.* Oxford: Oxford University Press.

Gross, Liz. 1986. *Irigaray and the Divine.* Sydney: Local Consumption.

Harris, Marvin. 1979. *Cultural Materialism: The Struggle for a Science of Culture.* New York: Random House.

Hastings, Margaret & Elisabeth G. Kimball. 1979. 'Two Distinguished Medievalists: Nellie Neilson and Bertha Putnam.' *The Journal of British Studies.* XVIII. 2 : 142–59.

Hawthorn, Jeremy. 1996. *Cunning Passages: New Historicism, Cultural Materialism and Marxism in Contemporary Literary Debate.* London: Arnold.

Hilton, Rodney. 1990. *Class Conflict and the Crisis of Feudalism.* London: Verso.

Hinderer, Drew W. 1982. 'On Rehabilitating Margery Kempe.' *Studia Mystica* 5.3: 27–43.

Hirsh, John C. 1975. 'Author and Scribe in *The Book of Margery Kempe.*' *Medium Aevum* XLIV: 145–150.

———1984. 'Margery Kempe.' *Middle English Prose: A Critical Guide to Major Authors and Genres.* Ed. A. S. G. Edwards. New Brunswick, N.J.: Rutgers University Press: 109–120.

———1988. *Hope Emily Allen: Medieval Scholarship and Feminism.* Norman, Oklahoma: Pilgrim Books.

Holbrook, Sue Ellen. 1985. 'Order and Coherence in *The Book of Margery Kempe.*' *The Worlds of Medieval Women: Creativity, Influence, Imagination.* Ed. Constance H. Berman, Charles W. Connell and Judith Rice Rothschild. Morgantown: West Virginia University Press: 97–112.

———1987. 'Margery Kempe and Wynkyn de Worde.' Ed. Marion Glasscoe. *The Medieval Mystical Tradition in England.* Cambridge: D. S. Brewer, 27–46.

———1992. '"About Her": Margery Kempe's Book of Feeling and Working.' eds. James M. Dean & Christian K. Zacher. *The Idea of Medieval Literature: New Essays in Honor of Donald R. Howard.* Newark: University of Delaware Press.

Horowitz, Helen Lefkowitz. 1994. *The Power and the Passion of M. Carey Thomas.* New York: Alfred A. Knopf.

Inge, W. R. 1959. *Mysticism in Religion.* London: Hutchinson.

Irigaray, Luce. 1986. *Divine Women*. Sydney: Local Consumption.

Johnson, Lynn Staley. 1991. 'The Trope of the Scribe and the Question of Literary Authority in the Works of Julian of Norwich and Margery Kempe.' *Speculum* 66: 820–38.

———1992. 'Margery Kempe: Social Critic.' *The Journal of Medieval and Renaissance Studies* 22.2: 159–194.

Jones, Rufus M. 1909. *Studies in Mystical Religion*. London: Macmillan.

Kelliher, Hilton. 1981. 'The Early History of the Malory Manuscript.' *Aspects of Malory*. Eds. Toshiyuki Takamiya and Derek Brewer. Woodbridge: Rowman and Littlefield, 1981: 143–157.

———1997. 'The Rediscovery of Margery Kempe: A Footnote.' *The British Library Journal*. 23.2: 259–63.

Kelliher, Hilton & Sally Brown. 1986. *English Literary Manuscripts*. London: British Library.

Klaus, H. Gustav. 1993. 'Cultural Materialism: A Summary of Principles.' Eds. W. John Morgan and Peter Preston. *Raymond Williams: Politics, Education, Letters*. London: St. Martin's Press.

Lie, Suzanne Stiver & Virginia E. O'Leary, eds. 1990. *Storming the Tower: Women in the Academic World*. London: Kogan Paul Ltd.

Lochrie, Karma. 1986. '*The Book of Margery Kempe*. The Marginal Women's Quest for Literary Authority.' *Journal of Medieval and Renaissance Studies* 16:1: 33–55.

———1991a. 'The Language of Transgression: Body, Flesh, and Word in Mystical Discourse.' Ed. Allen J. Frantzen. *Speaking Two Languages: Traditional Disciplines and Contemporary Theory in Medieval Studies*. Albany: State University of New York Press.

———1991b. *Margery Kempe and Translations of the Flesh*. Philadelphia: University of Pennsylvania Press.

Macherey, Pierre. 1978. *A Theory of Literary Production*. London: Routledge and Kegan Paul.

Mason, Mary Grimley & Carol Green Hurd, eds. 1979. *Journeys: Autobiographical Writings by Women*. Boston: G. K. Hall.

Matthews, David. 1999. *The Making of Middle English: 1765–1910*. Minneapolis: The University of Minnesota Press.

Mayakovsky, Vladimir. 1974. *How Are Verses Made?* trans. G. M. Hyde. London: Jonathan Cape.

McKenzie, D. F. 1986. *Bibliography and the Sociology of Texts*. [The Panizzi Lectures, 1985] London: The British Library.

Meech, Sanford Brown & Hope Emily Allen. 1940. *The Book of Margery Kempe*. EETS 212 O.S. London: Oxford University Press.

Milner, Andrew. 1993. *Cultural Materialism*. Melbourne: Melbourne UniversityPress.

Mitchell, Marea. 2001. '"The Ever-Growing Army of Serious Girl Students": The Legacy of Hope Emily Allen.' *Medieval Feminist Forum*, No 31, Spring: 17–29.

———2004. 'Uncanny Dialogues: The Journal of Mistress Joan Martyn and *The Book of Margery Kempe*.' Eds. Louise d'Arcens and Juanita de Ruys. *Maistresse of My Wit: Medieval Women and Modern Scholarship*. Turnhout, Belgium: Brepols, 247-66.

Morgan, W. John & Peter Preston. 1993. *Raymond Williams: Politics, Education, Letters*. London: St Martin's.

Mueller, Janel M. 1986. 'Autobiography of a New "Creatur": Female Spirituality, Selfhood, and Authorship in *The Book of Margery Kempe*.' Ed. Mary Beth Rose. *Women in the Middle Ages and the Renaissance*. Syracuse: Syracuse University Press, 155–171.

Mulhern, Francis. 1979. *The Moment of Scrutiny*. London: New Left Books.

Nemerov, Howard. 1977. 'A Poem of Margery Kempe.' *The Collected Poems of Howard Nemerov.* Chicago: University of Chicago Press.

Neuburger, Verena E. 1994. *Margery Kempe: A Study in Early Feminism.* Berne: Peter Lang.

Newman, Barbara. 1995. *From Virile Woman to WomanChrist.* Philadelphia: University of Pennsylvania Press.

Nordhoff, Charles. 1966. *The Communistic Societies of the United States: From Personal Visit and Observation.* New York: Dover.

Noyes, John Humphrey. 1966. *History of American Socialisms.* New York: Dover Publications.

Oakeshott, W. F. 1965. 'The Finding of the Manuscript.' Ed. J. A. W. Bennett. *Essays on Malory.* Oxford: Clarendon: 1–6.

O'Connell, Rev. Sir John R. 1937. 'Mistress Margery Kempe of Lynn.' *Downside Review* 5: 174–182.

Owst, G. R. 1961. *Literature & the Pulpit in Medieval England.* Oxford: Basil Blackwell.

Partner, Nancy. 1989. '"And Most of All for Inordinate Love": Desire and Denial in *The Book of Margery Kempe.' Thought: A Review of Culture and Thought* LXIV. 252: 254–267.

Partner, Nancy F. 1991. 'Reading *The Book of Margery Kempe.' Exemplaria* 3.1: 29–66.

————1993a. 'No Sex, No Gender.' *Speculum* 68: 419–443.

————1993b. 'Studying Medieval Women: Sex, Gender, Feminism.' *Speculum* 68: 305–308.

Passmore, S. Elizabeth. 'Painting Lions, Drawing Lines, Writing Lives: Male Authorship in the Lives of Christina of Markyate, Margery Kempe, and Margaret Paston,' *Medieval Feminist Forum*, No. 36, Fall 2003: 36–40.

Patterson, Lee, ed. 1990a. *Literary Practice and Social Change in Britain 1380–1530.* Berkeley: University of California Press.

————1990b. 'On the Margin: Postmodernism, Ironic History, and Medieval Studies.' *Speculum* 65: 87–108.

Pearsall, Derek. 1999. *From Chaucer to Spenser.* Oxford: Basil Blackwell.

Porter, Roy. 1988. 'Margery Kempe and the Meaning of Madness.' *History Today* February 38: 39–44.

Provost, William. 1984. 'The English Religious Enthusiast: Margery Kempe.' Ed. Katharina M. Wilson. *Medieval Women Writers.* Athens: University of Georgia Press: 298–319.

Robinson, Jane. 1991. *Wayward Women: A Guide to Women Travellers.* Oxford: Oxford University Press.

Rose, Mary Beth, ed. 1986. *Women in the Middle Ages and the Renaissance.* Syracuse: Syracuse University Press.

Ross, James Bruce & Mary Martin McLaughlin. 1977. *The Portable Medieval Reader.* Harmondsworth: Penguin.

Russ, Joanna. 1984. *How to Supress Women's Writing.* London: The Women's Press.

Sacks, Oliver. 1985. *The Man Who Mistook His Wife for a Hat.* London: Picador.

Scott, Joan Wallach. 1988. *Gender and the Politics of History.* New York: Columbia University Press.

Shils, Edward & Carmen Blacker. 1996. *Cambridge Women: Twelve Portraits.* Cambridge: Cambridge University Press.

Shillingsburg, Peter L. 1989. 'An Inquiry into the Social Status of Texts and Modes of Criticism.' *Studies in Bibliography* 42: 55–79.

Sinfield, Alan. 1992. *Faultlines: Cultural Materialism and the Politics of Dissident Reading.* Oxford: Oxford University Press.

Skinner, John. 1998. *The Book of Margery Kempe.* New York: Image.

Smith, Bonnie G. 1984. 'The Contribution of Women to Modern Historiography in Great Britain, France, and the United States, 1750–1940.' *The American Historical Review* 89.3: 709–32.

Spender, Dale. 1982. *Women of Ideas and What Men Have Done to Them: From Aphra Behn to Adrienne Rich*. London: Routledge & Kegan Paul.

Spiegel, Gabrielle M. 1990. 'History, Historicism, and the Social Logic of the Text in the Middle Ages.' *Speculum* 65: 59–86.

Staley, Lynn. 1994. *Margery Kempe's Dissenting Fictions*. Philadelphia: The Pennsylvania State University Press.

———2001. *The Book of Margery Kempe*. New York: W. W. Norton & Co.

Tepper, Sheri S. 1993. *Beauty*. London: Grafton.

Thornton, Martin (Priest of the Oratory of the Good Shepherd). 1960. *Margery Kempe: An Example in the English Pastoral Tradition*. London: Talbot, SPCK.

Thurston, Fr. [Herbert]. 1922. 'The Transition Period of Catholic Mysticism.' *The Month*: 526–537.

Thurston, Herbert. 1923. 'Pithiatism, Otherwise Called Hysteria.' *The Month*: 97–108.

———1928. Rev. of Hope Allen, *Writings Ascribed to Richard Rolle* (1927). *The Month*: 369–371.

———1936a. 'The Book of Margery Kempe.' *The Tablet*, October 24: 570–1.

———1936b. 'Margery the Astonishing.' *The Month* 2: 446–456.

———1955. *Surprising Mystics*. Chicago: Henry Regnery.

Triggs, Tony D. 1995. *The Autobiography of the Madwoman of God: 'The Book of Margery Kempe.'* Ligouri, Missouri: Triumph.

Wake, Joan, ed. 1943. *Northamptonshire and Rutland Clergy from 1500* by Rev. Henry Isham Longden. Northampton: Archer and Goodman.

Watkin, E. I. 1941. 'In Defence of Margery Kempe.' *The Downside Review*, LXIX 179: 243–63.

Whitson, Carolyn Elizabeth. 1994. *The Anatomy of Conflict: Gender and Strategies in 'The Book of Margery Kempe.'* Santa Cruz: University of California, Ph.D. thesis.

Williams, Raymond. 1965. *The Long Revolution*. Harmondsworth: Penguin.

———1977. *Marxism and Literature*. Oxford: Oxford University Press.

———1980. *Problems in Materialism and Culture: Selected Essays*. London: Verso and New Left.

———1981. *Culture*. Glasgow: Fontana.

Wilson, Scott. 1995. *Cultural Materialism: Theory and Practice*. Oxford: Blackwell.

Windeatt, Barry. 1984. *English Mystics of the Middle Ages*. Cambridge: Cambridge University Press.

———1985. *The Book of Margery Kempe*. Harmondsworth: Penguin.

———,ed.. 2000. *The Book of Margery Kempe*. Essex: Longman.

Worde, Wynkyn de, ed. 1501. 'A shorte treatyse...'. STC 14924.

Woolf, Virginia. 1984. *The Common Reader*, Volume I. Ed. Andrew McNeillie. London: The Hogarth Press.

———1985. ['The Journal of Mistress Joan Martyn.'] Ed. Susan Dick. *The Complete Shorter Fiction of Virginia Woolf*. London: The Hogarth Press.

Zacher, Christian K. 1976. *Curiosity and Pilgrimage: The Literature of Discovery in Fourteenth Century England*. Baltimore: Johns Hopkins University Press.

Zumthor, Paul. 1986. *Speaking of the Middle Ages*. Trans. Sarah White. Foreword by Eugene Vance. London: University of Nebraska Press.

 # INDEX

Numbers in bold refer to photographs